Heaven Begins
Within You

ANSELM GRUEN

Heaven Begins Within You

Wisdom from the Desert Fathers

Translated by Peter Heinegg

A Crossroad Book
The Crossroad Publishing Company
New York

First Published in the U.S.A. in 1999 by
The Crossroad Publishing Company
370 Lexington Avenue, New York, NY 10017

Original edition:
Der Himmel beginnt in dir:
Das Wissen der Wüstenväter für heute
Published by Herder Verlag, Freiburg im Breisgau, 1994

Printed in the United States of America

Library of Congress Cataloging-in-Publication Data
Gruen, Anselm.
  [Himmel beginnt in dir. English]
  Heaven begins with you : wisdom from the Desert Fathers / by
Anselm Gruen.
     p. cm.
  ISBN 0-8245-1818-7 (pbk.)
  1. Desert Fathers. 2. Spiritual life – Christianity – History of
doctrines – Early church, ca. 30-600. I. Title.
BR195.C5G7613 1999
248.4'811– dc21   99-16157

1 2 3 4 5 6 7 8 9 10   04 03 02 01 00 99

Contents

Introduction

Not long ago, while reading the news bulletin of a bank, I was surprised to see the author of the lead article on problems in business management start off with an old monastic tale. Evidently managers these days are finding help for their life and work in the sometimes strange-sounding *Apophthegmata* (that is, remarks of the fathers, sayings of the monks embedded in little anecdotes). Years ago the modern thing was to quote Zen Buddhist koans; now people are beginning to discover the wisdom of the fathers of the desert. Psychologists are taking an interest in the experiences of the early monks, in their methods of observing and dealing with thoughts and feelings. They sense that this isn't mere talk about humans and God, that the monks' words come from sincere self-knowledge and real experience of God.

The church today would do well to get in touch with the early sources of its spirituality. This would provide a better response to the spiritual longing of people than some moralizing theology trapped in the confines of the last two centuries. The spirituality of the early monks is mystagogical, that is, it leads one into the mystery of God and the mystery of being human. And just as ancient medicine saw its most important task in dietetics — the science of healthy living — so the monks understand their directives on asceticism and spirituality as an introduction to the art of healthy living. In the pages that follow we shall dip into the rich wellspring of spirituality as it was lived by the early monks from about the years 300 to 600.

Around the year 270 c.e., while attending the liturgy, the twenty-year-old Anthony heard the words of Jesus: "Go, sell what you have, and give to the poor, and you will have treasure in heaven; and come, follow me" (Mark 10:21). The words struck the young man to the heart. He sold his inheritance and went off into the desert. First he locked himself up in an abandoned fort, cut off from all contact with the outside world. There he was alone with God. But he encountered more than God; he encountered himself. And then he felt an uproar going on inside him. He was confronted with his shadow side. The people who passed by the fort heard some sort of tumult: it was the struggle with the demons, the fight with the forces of the unconscious, which were carrying on like wild animals. The demons hurled themselves at Anthony with a loud scream, but he stood up to them. Trusting in God's support, he withstood their onslaught. And when alarmed passers-by broke into the fort, they were met by a man who had been "initiated into profound mysteries and full of the spirit of God." As Athanasius writes in his famous biography: "The make-up of his inner life was pure. For he would become neither sullen in displeasure nor boisterous in his joy; nor did he have to struggle with laughter or bashfulness. For the sight of large crowds did not bewilder him; yet one never noticed any expressions of joy at being hailed by so many people. Rather he was completely even-tempered, as if he were led by his reflections and assured in his peculiar way. Through him the Lord healed many of those present who had bodily sufferings, and he set others free from demons. He also shared his friendly conversation with our Anthony. And thus he consoled many grieving persons. He reconciled others who were at odds with one another, so that they became friends."

Anthony withdrew still more deeply into the desert, but even there he did not remain alone. His example started a trend. Around the year 300 we find hermits everywhere in the desert, some of them disciples of Anthony. The longing to seek God in solitude as a monk evidently became so strong in this era that *kellia* (that is, small religious houses) came into existence, monastic cells that lay at some distance from one another. Around this time Christianity had become an established religion, and the power of faith was growing shallow. So the monks wanted to live the imitation of Christ in a radical fashion as "martyrs," that is, witnesses to faith. Thus the monastic movement arose in various places.

It had its roots in early Christian ascetical circles. The early church was, as a group, so otherworldly that one could almost say that everyone back then was a monk. In the second century ascetics formed the core of the communities around which believers gathered in order to continue living as Christians in the hostile atmosphere of the Roman empire.

Around the year 300 the first signs of the monastic movement began to appear. Monks settled down in various places, first in uninhabited regions, and then in the desert. Scholars are still arguing over the origins of monasticism. Obviously there were some non-Christian sources. The Bible itself issues no call to monastic life. Monasticism is a broadly human movement that can be found in all religions, a primordial longing to live for God alone, to prepare oneself, through asceticism and flight from the world, for union with God. Christian monks followed this longing, but they always interpreted it from the perspective of the Bible and found in the Bible a justification for their radical imitation of Christ. Greek philosophy also played a role. Some ideas and practices of the monks resemble, for example, those of the Pythagoreans. The connection of asceticism with mysticism, the vision of God, is typically Greek. The ascetical vocabulary comes, for the most part, from the language of Hellenistic popular philosophy" (Heussi, 292): asceticism, *anachoresis* (withdrawal from the world), monk (from *monachos,* someone who separates himself), coenobite (member of a monastic community), and many more.

Beginning around the year 300 monks withdrew into the wilderness from all the surrounding areas. They worked and prayed there the whole day long; they fasted and vied with one another in asceticism. They didn't invent asceticism but took over in their practices what they found already present in other religious movements. Without this knowledge their lonely life in the wilderness would have ended in psychic collapse and madness. The monks borrowed the wisdom and experience assembled earlier by ascetics from all religions and from philosophical circles. Only in this way could they endure their life in continuous isolation and vigils as well as in the constant search for God; and so they acquired a great knowledge of human nature and a real flair for God.

The monastic fathers turned into the psychologists of their day. In solitude they made careful observations of their thoughts and feelings and then discussed them on Sunday, when they came together and celebrated the Eucharist with their *abba* (spiritual father), so that their ascetical struggles wouldn't go astray. They talked about their thoughts and feelings, about their concrete way of life, and about their path to God. Thus there arose the so-called monastic confession, which was not primarily about forgiveness of sins, but about spiritual advising, the guidance of souls. This was an earlier form of the therapeutic dialogue developed by modern psychology. In any case a great many people, even from abroad, from Rome, for example, set out as pilgrims to visit the hermits who had withdrawn from the world and to seek their advice. Just as today great numbers of truth-seekers go on pilgrimage to the gurus in India, people from all over traveled into the Egyptian desert. They obviously sensed that there were men and women living there who understood something about being human and who spoke authentically about God, because they had experienced him.

In 323 Father Pachomios founded a monastery in the desert of Upper Egypt at Tabennisi. While the hermits before this had only a loose cohesiveness, Pachomios was the first one to found a community of monks, to which he gave a clear structure. Large monasteries took shape with over a thousand monks, tightly organized. These were the model for all the monasteries that gradually arose in both East and West, until they reached a historic high point with Benedict's founding of Monte Cassino. These monks wished to live the Christian faith in community. The longing for the primitive church, where, Luke tells us, all those who believed were of one heart and soul and held everything in common (Acts 4:32–33), led the monks to search for God in a life together.

The common bonds between rich and poor, between the various ethnic groups, became — at this chaotic time of national migrations — a sign that the kingdom of God had come. Although the monks had withdrawn from the world into the wilderness, they nonetheless left a deeper mark on the world than any other force of waning antiquity. Benedict of Nursia, who in the unsettled period of the migrations founded a small monastery on Monte Cassino, became the "Father of the West." The monasteries that followed his Rule shaped the culture of the West with their stress on prayer and work. They developed a clearly defined lifestyle that would mark Europe for long centuries to come.

As far back as the second half of the fourth century the monks were passing on the sayings of the great fathers. Even though these remarks had been made in concrete situations about specific problems, "the reader nevertheless sensed that the saying (*apophthegma* or apothegm) of the father, who had been filled with the Spirit, had a much more general and wide-ranging implication. Little collections of sayings were put together and disseminated throughout the Christian world. There are around 160 manuscripts in Greek alone" (*Weisung der Väter,* 17).

In the pages that follow we shall draw primarily from these sayings of the fathers. They seem to come from experience, never remaining theoretical. They offer guidance, and they are full of wisdom. But we shouldn't view the sayings of the fathers as some kind of universally valid maxims for the spiritual life. They are always addressed to a concrete case: they are meant especially for *this* questioner, as a therapeutic path for *this* particular person. Hence many sayings are one-sided and exaggerated. Here we don't have truths meant for everyone. The saying is intended for a given person in a given situation. They are designed as a stimulus to prompt that person to do what is necessary in the moment — instantly, today, this very day, not tomorrow.

The situation-oriented material handed down in the apothegms was described by Evagrios Pontikos (345–99) in a systematic fashion. Evagrios (or, in the more usual Latin form, Evagrius) was a Greek, a trained theologian, who got entangled in a love affair, fled from Constantinople, and became a monk. Directed by an elder to the monastic life, he soon became a much sought after spiritual father. Though always plagued by temptations, he turned out to be an expert in managing thoughts and feelings in the struggle with the demons. Many brothers looked him up and asked his advice in their spiritual battles. Thus Palladios, a disciple of Evagrius, writes: "His custom was as follows: the brothers would gather at his place on Saturday and Sunday. All through the night they would discuss their thoughts with him. They would listen to his powerful words till dawn. Then they would go away full of joy and praising God. For truly his instruction was very gentle."

At the request of many seekers of God Evagrius wrote down his experiences and thus provided an orientation for many monks in their spiritual struggles. His writings were always prompted by some occasion and composed for a particular petitioner. Palladios says about his books: "His intellect had become very pure; and he was blessed with the grace of wisdom and discernment in distinguishing the works of the demons. He was very well-versed in the Holy Scriptures and in the orthodox teachings of the Catholic Church. The books he wrote bear witness to his knowledge, wisdom, and exquisite understanding."

Over the centuries the writings of Evagrius became the intellectual foundation of monastic life. Unfortunately in the bitter campaign against Origen Evagrius fell into disfavor, and his writings were forbidden by the church. The monks solved this problem by attributing many of his books to St. Nilus. Thus despite ecclesiastical censorship they remained classics. In the West John Cassian (360–435), a disciple of Evagrius, wrote two books that preserved the wisdom of Evagrius for posterity. After the Bible, Cassian was the most widely read book in the Middle Ages.

The following chapters aim to present some aspects of ancient spirituality found in the sayings, Evagrius, Cassian, and other monastic authors, and in so doing to make them fruitful for our time.

Heaven Begins
Within You

ONE

Spirituality from Below

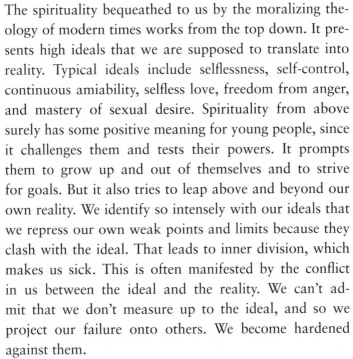

The spirituality bequeathed to us by the moralizing theology of modern times works from the top down. It presents high ideals that we are supposed to translate into reality. Typical ideals include selflessness, self-control, continuous amiability, selfless love, freedom from anger, and mastery of sexual desire. Spirituality from above surely has some positive meaning for young people, since it challenges them and tests their powers. It prompts them to grow up and out of themselves and to strive for goals. But it also tries to leap above and beyond our own reality. We identify so intensely with our ideals that we repress our own weak points and limits because they clash with the ideal. That leads to inner division, which makes us sick. This is often manifested by the conflict in us between the ideal and the reality. We can't admit that we don't measure up to the ideal, and so we project our failure onto others. We become hardened against them.

It's really amazing that very pious men and women can often react quite brutally, for example, when a theologian voices an opinion different from theirs. For example, in one diocese an art exhibit on the topic "Mary the Human

Being" was organized not long ago by a diocesan office, which led to the bishop's being subjected to brutal, even filthy attacks. But brutality is often repressed sexuality. Such people imagine they are defending the cause of piety; in fact they are behaving with im-pious militancy. Such representatives of a spirituality from above don't even notice that their arguments are hitting below the belt.

The desert fathers teach us a spirituality from below. They show us that we have to begin with ourselves and our passions. The way to God, for the desert fathers, always passes through self-knowledge. Evagrius Ponticus puts it this way: "If you want to know God, learn to know yourself first!" Without self-knowledge we are always in danger of having our ideas of God turn into mere projections. There are also pious individuals who take flight from their own reality into religion. They aren't transformed by their prayer and piety; they simply use it to lift themselves over others, to confirm their own infallibility.

In the desert fathers we meet an entirely different form of piety. The goals here are, above all, sincerity and authenticity. But this leads to affectionate understanding for all those who are not on the same path. Poimen, a tried and tested ancient father, once showed a great theologian the path to spirituality from below. The famous theologian wanted to engage Poimen in discussions about spiritual life and heavenly things, such as the Trinity. But Poimen just listened to him without saying a word. Stirred to anger, the theologian was about to walk out. Poimen's companion protested: "Father, this great man came here on account of you; he enjoys immense prestige back where he lives. Why haven't you spoken with him?" The old man replied: "He dwells on the heights and speaks of heavenly things; but I belong in the lower regions and speak of earthly things. If he had spoken about the passions of the soul, I would certainly have answered him. But when he talks about what is spiritual, I don't understand it."

The theologian was operating out of a spirituality from above. He spoke immediately about God and spiritual things. For Poimen the spiritual way began with the passions of the soul. These first have to be observed and struggled with. Only then will we understand something about God. For Poimen dealing with the passions was the path to God.

The theologian's encounter with Poimen ended with his disciple telling the irritated guest: "The old man does not speak readily about Scripture, but when someone speaks with him about the passions of the soul, he gives an answer." The guest thought for a while and went to him and said: "What should I do when the passions of the soul start overpowering me?" The old man gladly acknowledged him and said: "Now you've come the right way; open your mouth for these things, and I shall fill it with good." But the other found this very useful and said, "Truly, this is the right way!" And with gratitude to God he returned to his country, because he had been found worthy to meet with such a saint. Once they were talking about the passions of the soul, their conversation became sincere. They touched one another's hearts, and together they got into the subject of God, whom they suddenly felt in their midst, before their eyes, the goal of their path.

The following remark has been attributed to Anthony: "If you see that a young man is striving for heaven with his own will, grasp his feet and drag him down; for it will do him no good."

It makes no sense for young people to meditate too early on, to take the path to mysticism too soon. First they have to come to terms with their own reality. They have to take a good look at their passions and struggle with them. Only then can they head off on the inner path; only then can they attach their hearts completely to God. Today there are many people who have become fascinated too soon with spiritual paths. They think they can take these paths while skipping the difficult path of self-knowledge, the encounter with their own shadow side.

The monks warn us about spirituality that seeks to take heaven by storm: it can easily share the fate of Icarus, who made waxen wings and then plummeted when he came too close to the sun: they didn't support him. Some call the path taken by such high-flyers "spiritual bypassing." There's a serious risk of our using meditation to avoid the problems that we actually have to solve, such as repressed sexuality, hidden aggression, and anxiety. So when young people voice overly pious thoughts, I always try to have them look at the other side of things: concrete everyday life, work, school, study. I don't reject or ridicule pious thoughts and paths; that's not for me to do. And there's much sincere longing in their piety. But it's important that their piety keep its feet on the ground, that it penetrate their everyday life and work.

St. Benedict describes this spirituality from below in the chapter of his Rule on *humilitas*. He takes Jacob's ladder (Genesis 28) as an image for our way to God. The paradox of our spiritual path consists in the fact that we ascend to God by descending into our own reality. That is how Benedict understands Jesus' saying, "He who humbles himself will be exalted" (Luke 14:11, 18:14).

By descending into our earth-boundedness (humility is derived from *humus*, or soil) we come into contact with heaven, with God. When we find the courage to climb down into our own passions, they lead us up to God. This sort of humility was prized by the monastic fathers because it is the lower path to God, the path that leads through one's own reality to the true God. The heaven-stormers encounter only their own images of God, their own projections.

Isaac of Nineveh likewise used the image of Jacob's ladder as an image for the ascent to God through descent: "Strive to enter the treasure chamber that is within you; that way you will see the heavenly treasure. For the former and the latter are one and the same. By entering in you will see both. The ladder to the kingdom of heaven is hidden in your soul. Dive away from sin into yourself, and then you will find steps on which you can climb up."

We have to plunge through sin into our deepest foundation. Then we'll be able to climb up to God from all the way down. The ascent to God corresponds to a primordial longing of humanity. Plato's philosophy revolves precisely around this human ascent to God in the spirit.

The church fathers see in Jesus Christ, who first descended into hell before ascending into heaven (see Eph. 4:9), another model for our ascent to God. Like Jesus we first have to go down into our humanity before going up to God together with him.

Only the humble, who are prepared to accept their *humus,* their earth-bound condition, their humanity, their shadow, will experience the real God. Thus we keep hearing the monks praise humility. Humility is the path to God, and it is the clearest sign that we have gotten in line with God. Mother Theodora says: "Neither asceticism nor vigils, nor any laborious effort leads to salvation, only sincere humility....Look how humility conquers the demons!" And the devil who tangles with Makarios has to confess: "You are superior to me in one thing only." "And what is that?" Makarios asked. He answered: "Your humility. That is why I can't make any headway against you." And Poimen says: "Humans need humility and the fear of God, like the breath that issues from their nostrils."

For the monks humility is the courage to face the truth, the courage to accept their own earthliness, their humanity. The monks test one another in humility, so as to find out whether someone really is a man of God. "A monk was highly praised to Anthony by the brothers. Then Anthony took him and put him to the test, to see if he could endure insults. When it became clear that the man couldn't bear them, Anthony told him: You are like a village with a beautifully decorated facade, but behind it everything has been devastated by robbers."

"The saintly Synkletika used to say: 'Just as no one

can build a ship without nails, no person can become holy without humility.' " Humility is the test of whether one is living from the spirit of God. But it is also the foundation on which the monk builds his life. Without humility he always risks taking over God for his own purposes. Humility is the prerequisite for letting God be God, for developing a sense for God as the wholly other. The closer people come to God, the humbler they get. Then they can feel how far removed they are from God's holiness. Humility is the response to the experience of God.

Sometimes the monks also speak of the possibility of learning to be humble: "An old man was asked: 'What is humility?' And he answered: 'Humility is a great, indeed a divine work! But the way to humility is this: one should do physical labor; one should take oneself for a sinful person; one should be subject to everyone.' The brother asked: 'Does that mean subject to one and all?' The old man replied: 'That means, subject to everyone: when you do not heed the mistakes of others, but consider your own, and when you pray unceasingly to God.' "

Consequently the father suggests concrete exercises for the monks to learn humility. For us these exercises seem too negative. But, in the final analysis, they are about contemplating and accepting the truth about oneself instead of troubling oneself over the sins of others. And humility means following Christ in secret, not trumpeting the good I am doing for everyone to hear. Thus one old father says: "Just as a treasure, once it has been opened, is worth less, so a virtue made public lessens. For as wax melts from fire, the soul falls away from its pure estimation when it is dissolved by praise." And another monastic father: "It is impossible that plants and seeds bring forth at the same time. It is equally impossible that we should enjoy worldly fame and at the same time bring forth fruit for heaven." The fruits of the Holy Spirit can grow in us only when we give up showing them to everyone and pointing them out for all to see.

Spirituality from below points out that we come to God through careful self-observation and sincere self-knowledge. We don't find out what God wants from us in the lofty ideals we set for ourselves. Often these are merely the expression of our ambition. We wish to achieve high ideals to look better in the eyes of others and of God. Spirituality from below thinks that we can discover God's will for us, that we can find our vocation, only if we have the courage to descend into our reality and deal with our passions, our drives, our needs and wishes. The way to God leads through our weaknesses and powerlessness. When we are stripped of all power we discover what God has in mind for us, what God can make of us when God fills us completely with divine grace.

By contrast, spirituality from above reacts to the rage that boils up in us by repressing or crushing it: "Rage is not supposed to happen. As a Christian I've got to be friendly and balanced at all times. So I have to control my rage." Spirituality from below would mean questioning my rage, questioning what God wants to tell me with it. Perhaps my rage is pointing to some deep injury. Perhaps in my rage I encounter the wounded child in me that reacts with impotent fury to harm done to me by my parents or teachers. Perhaps my rage shows me that I have given others too much power over me. In that case rage would be the energy to free myself from the power of others, so as to open up to God. Thus rage isn't automatically bad; it could be showing me the way to my true self.

Through my rage I come into contact with myself, through the descent into my reality.

Through my rage I come into contact with the source of my strength, as God's spirit bubbles up within me. And so my rage leads me to God, who wishes to give me life. Rage defends me against everything that would take God's life away from me. Wherever my greatest problem lies is also the site of my greatest opportunities; that is where my treasure is. There I come into contact with my true essence. There is something that wants to come alive, to bloom.

The way to God leads through the encounter with myself, through the descent into my reality.

I have served as advisor to a nun who often got depressed. Whenever she supervised or criticized a fellow sister, she fell into an emotional hole. She had hoped that meditation would free her from her sensitivity and depression. But in our sessions it became clear that this was her own choice. She wanted to use God to make her look better in her own and others' eyes, to finally be liberated from her sensitivity. She wanted to use God for herself, to get over her depression by taking the path to God. But in our conversations it became clearer and clearer to her that this was the wrong way; and she discovered that she would find her way to God instead by the path of sorrow. When she lets herself into her feelings of depression, when she gets in touch with her total inability to overcome her sensitivity, when she admits that she has deeply wounded her fellow sisters, that they are simply hurting, then, on the basis of these feelings, on the basis of her powerlessness, she can suddenly experience a deep peace. Then she can let herself fall into God. She senses that she doesn't have to overcome her sensitivity at all. She is allowed to *be*. She gives up the struggle and surrenders to God. That makes her really free. She now meets the real God, the God who takes her out of the depths, who pulls her out of the deepest mud, the God who goes with her through fire and water. Then she is suddenly touched in her heart by God. All her own notions of God fall away, and she can sense the real God who bears her, frees her — and loves her.

Dorotheus of Gaza once said: "Your backsliding, says the prophet (Jer. 2:19), will teach you." The place where we slipped, where we fell away from God is where we learn a lesson of the kind that our virtues cannot teach us. The place where we meet our own powerlessness is precisely where we become open to God. God educates us through our failure, through our "backsliding." Then God guides us on the path of humility that alone leads to God.

Dorotheus believes that even when we fall "nothing happens without God.... God knew that it would be good for my soul, and that is why it came about this way. For in everything that God lets happen there is nothing pointless; on the contrary, everything everywhere is meaningful and purposeful." Everything has a meaning, even our passions, even our sins. They direct us more strongly than our discipline to God as the only guarantor of a successful life. We can't give any guarantee for ourselves. We will always fall again and again. But God leads us along the path beside all the cliffs, through all the backsliding and falling away.

The following chapters will discuss several aspects of this spirituality from below as it was lived by the early monks. It's important for me here to expound the themes of this spirituality while keeping an eye on our own time. At first glance many of the sayings of the ancient fathers may strike us as odd, and perhaps harsh and bitter too. But when we look and listen more carefully, they lead us into a world of love and compassion, of truth and freedom. They direct us into the mystery of God and humanity. That is why they are called mystagogical — they lead us into the mystery — and not moralistic. They don't insist on correctness.

After considering some typical subjects covered in the sayings of the fathers we will turn to the systematic presentations of Evagrius Ponticus, who offers the best summary of the spirituality of the desert fathers.

Two

Staying by Oneself

$$= \diamond =$$

The ancient fathers continually advise the monks to remain in their *kellion,* to hold out and not run away from themselves. *Stabilitas* — constancy, holding on, staying by oneself — is the condition for every kind of human and spiritual progress. St. Benedict sees in stability the cure for the sickness of his day (the time of the great tribal migrations), of uncertainty and constant movement. *Stabilitas* means remaining in the community that one has entered. And for Benedict it means that the tree must send down roots to be able to grow. Continual transplanting only blocks its development.

"Stability" means first of all staying by oneself, persevering before God in one's *kellion.* Father Serapion says: "Child, if you want to have success, then stay in your *kellion,* pay attention to yourself and your manual labor. Going outside will not bring you so much profit as sitting still."

The *kellion* means the monk's habitation, a small space that he has built for himself and normally spends all his time in. He sits there praying and meditating. He also works there and spends his time weaving baskets, which he sells once a month at the market. We keep hearing in ever new variations the advice that whatever else one does, one must not run away from oneself, but remain in the *kellion:* "A brother came into the skete [monks' settlement] to Father Moses and asked to have a word with him. The old man told him: 'Out, go to your *kellion,* and sit down, and the *kellion* will teach you everything.' "

"Someone said to Father Arsenios: 'My thoughts are torturing me; they tell me: you can't fast or work, so at least visit the sick; for that too is love.' But the old man, who knew the seed of the demons, said to him: 'Go and eat, drink and sleep and don't work, only don't leave your *kellion!*' For he knew that staying in the *kellion* straightens the monk out."

Such monks can do anything. They don't need to practice any asceticism. They don't even need to pray, provided they stay in their cells. If they do that, something in them will be transformed; they will find order within themselves. They will come face to face with all the inner chaos that surfaces in them. And they will give up trying to run away from it.

But it's not enough just to sit in one's *kellion.* Father Ammonas is reported to have said: "Someone might sit for a hundred years in a *kellion* without learning how to do it right." But how then should the monk sit in his *kellion?* Is the issue here bodily posture, a definite way of sitting in meditation that keeps one awake? Or is the point the inner attitude one has while sitting in the *kellion?*

Presumably Father Ammonas means the attitude of *stabilitas,* of constancy. He's not talking about sitting to weave daydreams or to doze, but sitting before God, and persevering in God's presence. In sitting we become immobile. However many things may be stirring within us, even if our thoughts storm back and forth, we remain unmoved; we stand firm. And if we maintain this external rest, the storm of thoughts and feelings will calm down.

The inner attitude with which monks are supposed to sit in their cells is described by another elder in a drastic image: "When you dwell in the desert as a hesychast [a person who practices quietistic meditation], don't imagine that you are doing something great. Instead, think of yourself as a dog that has been driven away from the crowd and tied up because he bites and bothers people." The monks do not remain sitting in their cells because they think they are better than the men and women in the world. Rather they withdraw into their cells in order to protect the world from themselves. They are working on a sort of environmental protection for the mind. On the small site of their cells they do waste removal for the world by cleaning up anger and resentment. That way they create a purer atmosphere, an atmosphere of love and compassion.

The monks knew about the dangers of distraction. There is also spiritual distraction, a state where one runs through many thoughts about God and spiritual life. But with all those thoughts one never really touches God. Remaining in one's cell, keeping to oneself, is the necessary condition for both spiritual progress and maturation as a human being. One cannot be a mature person without the courage to hold out and meet one's own truth head on. A story told about one of the fathers compares staying in one's cell to smooth water in which one can more clearly make out one's face: "Three students who loved each other became monks, and each one of them undertook a good work. The first one had this story: he wanted to get disputants to make peace, in keeping with the words of Scripture: Blessed are the peacemakers. The second wished to visit the sick; the third went into the desert to live there quietly. The first monk, who worked with those who had quarreled, couldn't reconcile them all. Filled with despondency, he went to the second, who served the sick, and found that he too was depressed; for he too had failed to carry out his intentions completely. So they both agreed to look up the third, who had gone off into the desert. They told him about their problems and asked him to tell them frankly what he had achieved. He was silent for a while; then he poured some water into a vessel and told them to look in. But the water was still churned up. After a while he again had them look in and said: 'Now observe how placid the water has become.' They looked in and saw their faces as if in a mirror. Then he said: 'That is how it is with those who dwell among people: because of all the unrest and confusion they can't see their sins. But those who stay quiet, especially in solitude, will soon catch sight of their errors.' "

This is not meant to condemn love of one's neighbor. Rather the story points to the danger that may lurk in the wish to help others: we imagine that we can help the whole world. However, that is often a cover for a feeling of omnipotence. In all that we do there still remains, as always, the need for perseverance, for remaining in one's cell, and keeping silence. That makes the water in the vessel calm and smooth, and we can recognize our truth in it.

Remaining in one's cell is supposed to lead to two results: self-knowledge and complete concentration on God. "Father Anthony said: 'It is very good for us to seek refuge in our cell, and to reflect a great deal about ourselves during our life, until we learn what sort of persons we are. If you persevere in your cell, then you pay attention to your death. If you pray constantly night and day, then you will await your death.' "

A brother asked Anthony: "How should one remain sitting in one's cell, my father?" The old man answered: "What people can see is the fasting till evening, every day, the vigils, and meditation. But what remains hidden to men and women is the contempt of oneself, the struggle against evil thoughts, gentleness, the contemplation of death and the humility of the heart, the foundation of all that is good."

Makarios the Great said: "What is needful for monks sitting in their cells is that they should collect their understanding far from all worldly cares, without letting themselves wander around in the vanities of this world, that they should strain toward a single goal, their thoughts constantly directed to God, remaining always concentrated, allowing no worldly distraction into their hearts, neither carnal imaginings nor cares about their parents, nor consolation from their families, but that their mind and all their senses remain in the presence of God, so as to fulfill the saying of the Apostle: let the virgin be very close to the Lord, completely free from distraction" (1 Cor. 7:34).

Fourteen hundred years later Blaise Pascal saw the cause of human wretchedness in the fact that people couldn't bear staying in their rooms alone. Nowadays, for the most part, we still can't hold out, as we hop from one thing to another. It's so easy to find distraction — we need only channel-surf. But what is happening in the soul? Nothing can ripen anymore, nothing can grow, no truth takes place. Maturity calls for quiet. The *kellion* leads us into the truth. It confronts us with our own truth. But that is the precondition for all human maturity — and for healthy life together.

For the early monks, however, encounter with oneself was also the precondition for every authentic encounter with God. Our piety suffers when we dodge ourselves. In the case of many pious individuals one senses that they are using religion to avoid their own truth. They take refuge in pious thoughts and feelings so they won't have to encounter themselves. Many of them are fearful of meeting the self, and this translates into a fear of psychology. They damn the obsessive navel-gazing and propose loving God as an alternative.

But one often gets the impression that such persons have not made that much progress in the love of God, that this cursing of psychology doesn't deepen piety but simply derives from fear of the truth about themselves. In spiritual conversations I often get the feeling that some pious thoughts are meant well, but don't really add up. There are some who take refuge in such thoughts, in pious-sounding arguments. But they don't have the courage to look their thoughts in the eye.

The monks' spirituality is sincere. It doesn't vault over

human reality. Instead, the path to God passes through self-encounter. The monks don't talk about God; they experience God. They remove all possible distractions in order to orient their minds wholly and completely to God. If I stay in my cell, without doing anything, without having pious thoughts, without reading anything, then I sense what reality is. I can no longer have any pretensions, either about myself or my relations with God.

I may be able to speak and write eloquently about my relationship with God. But when everything is taken away from me and I really sit in all simplicity before God, then the idea occurs to me, first, that everything is boring. Or I begin to suspect that everything I've been saying about God doesn't add up. If I weather this feeling, if I don't immediately worry about being able to write something, but simply stay put, then something moves within me, then I will touch the truth. The truth is at first relentless, but it also sets us free.

Thus, staying in one's cell is a reality check, a test to see whether my life and my image of God make sense, whether my love for God is genuine. In my cell I no longer have the possibility of diverting myself, of seeking refuge in activities, of sailing off into daydreams. I have to take a stand. Then God presses in on me. God challenges everything that I have thought up about him and about my life.

In the Middle Ages the monks were forever singing the praises of the cell. They said, "Cella est coelum," the cell is heaven, where the monks converse familiarly with God, where God's presence envelops them. Then there is the formula "Cella est valetudinarium," the cell is an infirmary, a place where the sick can get better. It is a place of wholeness, a place for healing, because we sense God's loving and healing nearness there. But I can have this positive experience of the cell only if I stay there even when everything in me rebels against it, when I am full of unrest. Once I have overcome this first phase, then I may experience the cell as heaven. Heaven opens before me, my narrow cell breathes the expanses of heaven, because God dwells there.

THREE

The Desert and Temptation

One of the great themes of monasticism is the desert. The monks deliberately went into the desert to be alone and to seek God. The ancients considered the desert the dwelling-place of demons. Anthony went into the desert to fight the demons on their own turf. It was a heroic decision to push his way into the realm of the demons — and a declaration of war on the demons that plagued him and sought to drive him from their domain. Anthony believed that thanks to his struggle against the demons the situation for men and women in the world would be a little brighter and healthier. If he conquered the demons, then they would have less power over people in the world. To that extent his struggle with the demons was also fought on the world's behalf.

In the desert Anthony combated the demons as part of his service to humanity. It was his contribution toward improving the world. Having fled the world, he committed himself to the fight against the demons to make it healthier. For Anthony the desert was the place where the demons showed themselves more clearly and undisguisedly. Just as Jesus was tempted by the devil in the desert when he was led there by the Holy Spirit, the monks who went to the desert had to reckon with the fact that they would be forced to fight the demons. Human beings are essentially battlers. And the old fathers won praise when they were victorious in their struggle.

When the devil left Jesus alone, angels came and ministered to him. The mountain of temptation became the mountain of paradise. The monks had the same experience. The desert is not just the stamping ground of the demons, the place where one cannot hide from one's own truth, where one is unsparingly confronted with oneself and one's shadow side. The desert is also the place of the greatest closeness to God. Israel experienced this when it discovered the wilderness as the place where God was nearest. God led Israel through the desert so that the people might enter the Promised Land.

Thus the monks were led by God into the desert to endure the battle with the demons and through that struggle to come into the land of peace, into the land where one sees God. For Israel the wilderness was a time of testing and of the glorification of God. Looking back on its history Israel recognized the years in the wilderness as a privileged time. It was the time when God grew fond of Israel, took her in his arms, and drew her with the chains of love (see Hosea 11). And God promised Israel that he would lead her into the wilderness again, to speak to her heart. The time in the wilderness would then be a new honeymoon: "Therefore, behold, I will allure her, and bring her into the wilderness, and speak tenderly to her" (Hos. 2:14).

So the monks experienced the desert as a place where they were close to God, where they could sense God's love more intensely, because there were no worldly enticements to get in their way. But to sense the nearness of God, the monk has to take up the struggle with the demons. That struggle brings many temptations along with it, and temptation is where the monk meets the demons. The monks found that their strength and inner clarity grew by proving themselves in temptation and triumphing over the demons.

Temptation was part and parcel of their lives. Anthony says: "This is the great task of man, that he should hold his sin before the face of God, and count upon temptation until his last breath."

Human life is marked by constant conflict. We can't just float through life. We have to confront the temptations that life brings with it. And there will never be a time when we can rest on our laurels. Temptations will be with us till the point of death. In another passage Anthony says: "No one can make it to the kingdom of heaven untempted. Take away the temptations, and no one will find salvation." Anthony obviously saw temptations as the condition for entering the kingdom of heaven. Through them people get a sense for the true God. Without them we would be in danger of diminishing God or taking God over for our own purposes. In temptation we have an existential feeling of our distance from God and of the difference between humans and God. The human being always has to struggle, while God rests in himself. God is absolute love, whereas humans are constantly under assault by evil.

The monks saw temptations in a very positive light. One of the fathers put it this way: "If the tree isn't shaken by the winds, it doesn't grow and it bears no roots. It's the same with the monk: if he is not tempted and doesn't weather temptation, he will never become a man."

It's like the parable of the palm tree: an evil man became angry with a beautiful young palm tree. In order to damage it, he put a large stone in its crown. But when he passed by some years later, he found the palm tree had grown larger and more beautiful than all the others around it. The stone had forced it to send its roots more deeply into the earth. And thus it was able to grow higher. The stone became a challenge. Thus temptations are challenges for the monks. They force the monks to send down their roots more deeply into God, to put their trust more thoroughly in God. They show them that they can't get rid of temptations on their own. The constant confrontation makes them stronger inside and lets them mature into adulthood.

The struggle with temptations and trials is an essential part of being human. We must deal with the fact that we are tempted by our passions. The monks speak of demons fighting with us. By that they mean the forces that emerge in us, that pull us one way or another, that we do not consciously want. They focus on the experience that we are not simple and straightforward, that we are tossed here and there by various thoughts and feelings. And they use those terms to describe the forces that we have buried in our shadow side, the unconscious. Despite our attempt to be decent, the thought occurs to us to throw everything overboard, to simply dispense with the commandments. For all our amiability we sometimes think that what we'd really like to do is kill our neighbor. It would be naive to say that it's enough to keep the commandments and to will the good. There is a raging conflict in our heart between good and evil, between light and darkness, between love and hatred. For the monks this is perfectly normal. It's not wrong; it's the test that makes us tried and true. Nowadays we might say that it's a way to live with greater awareness. The monks know about their shadow side; they come to terms with the fact that their unconscious harbors forces that they do not know yet, that they have to be careful with.

Temptations, the monks tell us, make us human. They bring us into contact with the roots that bear the trunk. Facing temptations means encountering the truth. Thus one father says: "Take away temptations, and no one will be whole, for whoever flees useful temptation, flees eternal life. There are in fact temptations that have prepared crowns for the saints."

Many people might have problems with this, because when they pray the Our Father, they ask God, "Lead us not into temptation." But here Jesus is talking about a different kind of temptation, the temptation to fall away altogether. Let us not fall into the situation of breaking away. Thus Jesus teaches his disciples to pray, while he himself prays for them on that account (see Luke 22:31–32; John 17:14–15). On the contrary, by temptations the monks mean thoughts in our mind, passions, and demons. These temptations are an essential part of us. They test us, try us, and leave us the better for it.

But this also means that we can't come to God with a clean slate. Our task is rather to take part in the fight with the demons and to be wounded over and over again by it.

The monks don't insist that we be perfect and flawless, correct and without stain. Those who get to know the demons in temptation will encounter the truth of their souls. They will discover in themselves the abyss of the unconscious: murderous thoughts, sadistic imaginings, immoral fantasies. We become mature persons only when we confront these truths, when we prove ourselves in temptation.

Thus one father says: "When we pray to the Lord: Lead us not into temptation! (Matt. 6:13), we are not asking not to be tempted, because that would be impossible. We are asking only that we be not swallowed up in temptation and do something that displeases God. *That* is what not falling into temptation means."

Temptation brings us closer to God. That is how Isaac of Nineveh saw it: "Without temptation there is no way of perceiving God's care for us, there is no gaining trust in him, or learning the wisdom of the spirit, or solidifying the love of God in the soul. Before temptations you pray to God as if you were a stranger. After you have withstood the temptation out of love for him, without letting yourself be led astray by them, God looks upon you as one who has lent to him and who is entitled to the interest, and as a friend who has fought for his will against the power of the enemies." His words show that the monks had no anxiety about temptation or about sin. The monks who fall into temptation become familiar with God in a new way. At the same time in temptation they sense the nearness of God more deeply than usual.

Temptation keeps the monks awake and makes them continue growing within. Thus John Kolobos even begs for temptation so as to make progress on his way to God. Father Poimen used to say about Father John Kolobos: "He called upon God, and his passions were taken from him, and he had no cares. He went away and said to an old man: 'I notice that I am in peace and no longer have any temptations.' The old man said to him: 'Go and call upon God that an enemy may rise up against you, so that the old contrition and humility you used to have may return again! For it is precisely through temptation that the soul makes progress.' So he asked, and when the enemy came, he no longer prayed to be liberated from him. Instead he would say: 'Give me patience, Lord, in my struggles!' "

Without temptation the monks become careless. They let themselves go, and so live any old way. Temptations force them to live consciously, to exercise discipline, and to be wakeful. Thus the monks don't pray for temptations to stop, but for God to give them enough strength. "The story was told of Mother Sarrha, that for thirteen years she endured being violently assaulted by demons of impurity. She never prayed for the struggle to cease, but rather: 'O God, give me strength.' " Yet in the end she won. "The impure spirit said to her: 'You have conquered me, Sarrha.' But she answered: 'It is not I who have won, but my Lord Christ.' "

Temptation forces us to fight. Without a fight there

is no victory. But victory is never something we have earned. In our struggles we learn that Christ is working with us, that he frees us from endless conflict and gives us a profound peace.

The question is whether this positive view of temptation can help us today. For one thing, this perspective might liberate us from a false striving for perfection. Those for whom everything depends upon being correct will miss out on life for fear of making some mistake. Their lives will atrophy. They will, it is true, be correct, but not vital and capacious. Coming to terms with temptation, the certainty that temptation is part of us, makes us more human, or, as the monks say, humbler. It shows us that we are always under attack, that we can never claim to stand above all temptations, that hatred and jealousy, say, or adultery are no problem for us. Anyone who maintains that he would never betray his wife or girlfriend has not yet encountered his own heart. Coming to terms with temptation makes us alert.

But nowadays we have a hard time with the idea of the monks' begging God *not* to take temptation away from them. Nevertheless even today some people have had a similar experience. A nun told me that once masturbation ceased to bother her, she slackened off internally. So long as she had to fight against it, she was more attentive to her feelings, she dealt more consciously with frustration and anger. And she felt that she was wholly and entirely cast upon God. Her prayer became more intense.

We sometimes have a false image of holiness. We think that the saints are beyond all temptations, but that's wrong. Knowing about temptation without being overpowered by it is a way that keeps us alive, that continually reminds us that we cannot make ourselves better, that only God can transform us. Only God can give us the victory in the battle with temptations, can bring us a profound peace that can't be experienced as intensely without a struggle.

FOUR

Asceticism

The monks are forever talking about the struggle that life with God demands. Life in the wilderness is a continuous combat with the demons, and it demands constant effort from the monks. Mother Synkletika said: "Those who go to God have at first struggles and many hardships. But afterward the joy is unspeakable. Just as those who wish to light a fire are first bothered by the smoke and have to cry, but in this way reach their desired goal — for it is written: 'Our God is a consuming fire' (Heb. 12:29) — so we too must kindle the divine fire in us with tears and troubles."

"A brother asked Father Arsenios for a word. Arsenios said to him: 'Struggle with all your might, so that your inner effort may be in accord with God, and you will conquer your outer passions.'"

Father Zachariah was once asked what made a monk, whereupon he replied: "I think, Father, that whoever does violence to himself in all things is a monk."

In another apothegm Christ himself says to a monk: "'But I tell you: much toil is needed, and without toil no one can have God.' For he himself was crucified for us."

We have a hard time with such remarks, which promise us struggle and toil. One might think that the monks won't allow us to live, that all they see is harshness and renunciation. But in the final analysis behind the insistence on asceticism lies a positive image of humanity. The monks believe that we can work on ourselves. We aren't completely at the mercy of our predispositions or our past upbringing. The monks don't try to find excuses for themselves in an education gone wrong; they don't put the blame for their lives on other people. They take personal responsibility for their lives and shape them in the light of that responsibility. They don't feel helplessly abandoned to their desires. Instead they trust the power that God has given us, a power by which we can liberate ourselves from the obstacles that might hold us back from life.

Today we have once again an understanding for asceticism. The physicist and philosopher of nature Carl Friedrich Weizsäcker speaks of an ascetical global culture that is vitally necessary for the future of our planet. I was once invited by Austrian Television to a roundtable discussion on "The Passion for Asceticism." Alongside me sat two psychologists, a man and a woman, and a business executive. At first I thought I would have to defend asceticism. But we all agreed how important asceticism is today, as a way to freedom, as a way of taking control of one's own life and shaping it. In making this case we mustn't confuse asceticism with killing off feelings. Asceticism actually means exercising so as to obtain a skill. In the ethical sense asceticism is "practice in virtuous behavior corresponding to the ideal." Thus asceticism means something positive, exercising in order to acquire a religious behavior.

Not until the age of Stoic and Cynic popular philosophy did asceticism come to be viewed as renunciation and repression of drives. Christian ascetics put too much emphasis on this negative aspect, while with the monks the accent is placed on exercise, through which we train ourselves in *apatheia*, a condition of inner peace, in which we are open to God. For the monks, however, peace always comes out of struggle. Hence it's important, first of all, that we take up the struggle against the demons that would hold us back from God.

What Evagrius calls *apatheia* is for his disciple Cassian, who reformulated Evagrius's teaching in Latin, *puritas cordis*, or purity of heart. This is a condition of inner clarity and purity, of love as openness for God. To achieve purity of heart, we have to struggle. We must do all the actions that we perform by way of asceticism for purity of heart, in other words for love. These are the instruments that can free our hearts from all the harmful passions that prevent us from ascending to the full measure of love. Thus we practice fasting, vigils, seclusion, meditation on Holy Scripture, etc. for the sake of purity of heart, which consists in love. Whatever we do we do in order to become lovers. For this reason love sets the standard in everything. Achieving love is the goal of our activity; the tools that we use to get there are of secondary importance. Thus the goal of asceticism is something absolutely positive: the attainment of love, of purity of the heart. The main point is not renunciation, but love, which is attained by struggling against the passions. We see here a distinctly positive view of human life.

The monks developed methods for practicing the attitude of love, inner clarity and purity, and openness to God. In the monastic writings we find two recurrent images for our struggle to reach a life that we live ourselves, a life that corresponds to God's image of us: we are the athletes of Christ and the soldiers of Christ the King.

The monks are athletes of Christ. Their struggle is fought above all against the passions. But, unlike athletes in the arena, they will never permanently conquer their opponents, so they can't rest on their laurels. Rather our life is a continuous fight. The fathers urge young monks on to this struggle. One can sense the joy of battle in many of their sayings, which express the feeling that we are not abandoned to the demons, that we can conquer through the power of Christ. This chance to triumph inspires the monks in their struggle. Evagrius speaks of the monk who renounces his possessions as an athlete who "cannot be tackled around the waist, and a rapid runner who hastens to the prize of the calling from above."

According to Evagrius, however, we cannot win the battles against the passions unless "we stand in the battle as strong men and soldiers of our victorious king Jesus Christ. . . . Of course, in this battle we need as spiritual weapons a strong faith and solid teaching, that is, perfect fasting, powerful deeds, humility, scarcely disturbed or completely undisturbed silence, and unbroken prayer. But I would like to know if there are any who can carry out the struggle in their soul and can be crowned with the crown of justice if they satisfy their souls with bread and water, foment anger, despise and neglect prayer, and

meet with the heretics. For, behold, Paul says: 'Every athlete exercises self-control in all things' (1 Cor. 9:25)....
And so it is certainly fitting that when we undertake this campaign we put on our spiritual armor and show the heathen that we will fight against sin to the point of bloodshed."

Cassian challenges us to command our thoughts and passions, after the manner of the centurion of Capernaum: "We too can attain the rank of a spiritual centurion; we can hold our own amid the turbulence of our thoughts, create order among them thanks to the power of the gift of discernment [*discretio*], subject the disorderly crowd of our thoughts to the sovereignty of our reason, and beneath the saving sign of victory of our Lord's cross drive off all cruel enemies from within us. If we attain the rank of centurion, we shall have such power to command that thoughts will not be able to divert us from the path; and we can abide with those that spiritually delight us. Then we shall simply order the evil suggestions 'Begone!' and they will be gone, but tell the good ones 'Come!' and they will come. We shall also, like that centurion in the Gospel, be able to command our servant, that is, our body, to do everything needed for continence and chastity; and he will obediently serve us — meaning that he will no longer stir at the proddings of desire, but will follow the orders of the spirit."

In such statements we sense a lust for battle. Admittedly, asceticism is difficult for the monks, but it also brings joy. For in struggling the monks become stronger. But they are inspired above all by the goal of the struggle: entry into the land of peace, the attainment of *apatheia*, health of the soul, the experience of inner freedom, an unhampered love, and oneness with God.

Asceticism consists first in making the body docile and subjecting it to our will, becoming master of our drives, free from the demands of our needs.

To begin with, the subjection of the body to the spirit takes place in the ascetical control of diet. The monks give up meat; they eat as little as possible. Many fast and eat only every other day. But the monks also constantly warn about exaggerated fasting. The royal way is to eat once a day, and only a little in the evening, so that one doesn't become full. Asceticism relates to sleep as well. The monks wished to sleep as little as possible. Cutting down on sleep was already customary among the Pythagoreans. And many other spiritual movements use this method. The fatigue it induces was seen as a prerequisite for experiencing God intensively. When I am tired, I am not very receptive. When I concentrate my lowered receptivity entirely on God, I am more open to God than in complete wakefulness. But for the monks night too was an important place for the experience of God. In the night God visits humans and speaks to their hearts. It is a widely shared experience that we are closer to God at nighttime than during the day.

However, the monks keep warning against carrying asceticism too far, of wanting to subject one's body with no regard to one's own limits. Thus Anthony says: "There are some who have destroyed their bodies with penitential exercises. But because they lacked the gift of discernment, they drove themselves far from God." And Mother Synkletika says: "There is an exaggerated asceticism that is from the enemy. For his disciples make use of it too. How, then, do we distinguish the divine, royal asceticism from the tyrannical and demonic kind? Evidently through moderation."

Asceticism must not turn into a raging against oneself. Then it would only harm us. Poimen notes that "all excess is from the demons." Asceticism must also not be applied in the belief that we can redeem ourselves. It is, instead, a response to God's love, to God's offer of salvation in Jesus Christ. If God is to transform us through his word and his Spirit, we must hold ourselves out to him; we must free ourselves from everything that weighs us down internally, locks us up, and rules over us. But God alone can work our salvation. Thus the monks are aware of the paradox that we must indeed work hard on ourselves, but that basically we cannot make ourselves better through our own efforts. Only God can do that. Thus in asceticism the monks keep experiencing their own powerlessness. They can't drag themselves out of the swamp. They learn what grace is precisely when they reach a limit in their struggle. Then they sense that God alone can give them the victory, can grant them true peace and lasting love.

FIVE

Keeping Silence,
Not Passing Judgment

One sign that asceticism has led a monk to God is the refusal to pass judgment. However severely monks fast and however hard they work, all of that is useless if they nonetheless go on judging others. Asceticism has merely gotten them to the point where they can exalt themselves over others. It has served to satisfy their pride, to heighten their feeling of self-worth. Those who have encountered themselves in their asceticism, those who have persevered in remaining in their *kellion* when repressed thoughts and desires raise their head, will lose all appetite for judging others. That is why many sayings of the fathers admonish the monks to stay by themselves, to confront their own truth, and not to judge others.

Father Poimen asked Father Joseph: "Tell me how I become a monk." He answered: "If you wish to find peace, say whenever you do anything: 'I — who am I?' and judge no one!"

Theodore of Pherme says: "Anyone who has come to know the sweetness of the *kellion* flees from his neighbor, but without despising him." And: "A father was once asked by a brother: 'Why is it that I pass judgment on my brothers so frequently?' And he answered him: 'Because you don't yet know yourself. Whoever knows himself doesn't see the brothers' mistakes.' "

Passing judgment on others is always a sign that one has not yet encountered oneself. Hence pious individuals who become incensed over others have not yet encountered their own truth. Their piety has not yet confronted them with themselves and their own sin. For as Father Moses says: "If anyone is bearing his sins, he does not look on those of his neighbors."

But for the monks refusing to pass judgment is not only a criterion for genuine asceticism; it's also a help in finding one's inner peace. When we stop condemning others, that does *us* good.

"Poimen was asked by a brother: 'What should I do, Father, for I am becoming cast down by sadness.' The old man answered him: 'Do not look upon anyone for any reason; condemn no one, calumniate no one, and the Lord will give you rest.' "

Judging gives us no rest. For even while we are condemning the other, we unconsciously sense that we too are not perfect. Thus, renouncing judgment and condemnation is a way to inner peace with ourselves. We let others be as we are, and in this way we can also be ourselves.

With their experience the monks are carrying out what Jesus demands in the Sermon on the Mount: "Judge not, that you be not judged" (Matt. 7:1). Not-judging comes out of the encounter with the self. Those who have encountered themselves know all about their own errors.

They know their shadow side. They know that they bear within themselves what they condemn in others. When the others sin, they do not get indignant; they are reminded of their own sins. Psychologists tell us that when we pour abuse on others we are revealing what is in ourselves. We project our own shadow side, our repressed wishes and needs, onto others; and so we revile them instead of looking our own truth in the eye. The monks demand that we give up projection and be silent instead. Silence for them is an aid in giving up projection and viewing others' behavior as a mirror for ourselves. We can see this in a number of sayings by the fathers.

Father Poimen used to say, "It is written: 'What your eye has seen, that you shall attest to' (Prov. 25:7). But I say to you: 'Even if you grasp it with your hands, do not speak about it.' One brother was fooled in this matter. He saw something that looked as if his brother were sinning with a woman. Strongly tempted, he went over and kicked them with his foot, believing that it was they, and said; 'Stop it now! How long will you continue?' And behold, they were sheaves of grain. That is why I tell you: 'Even if you can grasp it with your hands, do not judge.' "

Poimen knew that we can project our own fantasies even into nature. The brother of whom he speaks was projecting his sexual desires onto the sheaves of grain. He saw in them what he had continually been imagining to himself. So mistrustful was Poimen of all judging that he even forbids us to do it when we think we could grasp the other's sin with our two hands. Even there, often enough, we are just grasping our own fantasies.

Silence means renouncing every projection. "When Father Agathon saw something and his heart wished to pass judgment on the thing, he would tell himself: 'Agathon, don't do it.' And thus his thinking came to rest." "If you see someone sinning, pray to the Lord and say: 'Forgive me if I have sinned.'"

Passing judgment on others makes us blind to our own mistakes. Silence while looking at others makes clear self-consciousness possible. We stop projecting our mistakes onto others. Thus one of the sayings reads: "In the skete there was an assembly once on account of a fallen brother. The fathers spoke; only Father Pior kept silent. Afterward he stood up, took a sack, filled it with sand, and carried it on his shoulder. Meanwhile he bore in front of him a little basket with a tiny amount of sand. The fathers asked him what that meant, and he answered: 'This sack with all the sand is my sins. I have put them behind me so that they won't worry me, and I won't weep over them. And behold, the few errors of my brother are in front of me, and I say all sorts of things to condemn him. It is not right to do so. Rather I should carry my own in front of me and think about them and beg God to forgive them.' Then the fathers stood up and said: 'Truly this is the way of salvation!'"

This sort of symbolic action can make it clearer to us how often we are on the point of condemning others. Perhaps we think that we are discussing another person out of concern for that person's salvation. In reality we are making a great to-do about that person's sins, while our own are much greater. But we simply won't admit it. Here we need a Father Pior to make it clear to us in a friendly, careful fashion that it makes no sense to get excited about other people's sins. It would be better to pray for them instead and to sense in prayer that we are all tempted, that none of us can guarantee that we will remain without mistakes.

Even when a brother really does sin, we shouldn't condemn him. Thus Poimen says: "When a person sins and denies it, claiming, 'I have not sinned,' do not condemn him. Otherwise you discourage him. But if you say, 'Do not lose heart, brother, in the future be careful!' you awaken his soul to repentance." Instead of condemning others, we should win them over to the love of God.

"The story was told about Father Isidore, the elder of the skete: If someone had a recalcitrant or weak brother, a neglectful or arrogant one, and wished to cast him out, he would say, 'Bring him to me!' And he would receive him and save him through his patience."

Again and again the monks sing the praises of silence. For them silence is the way to encounter themselves, to discover the truth of their own hearts. But silence is also the way to become free from constantly judging and condemning others. We are always in danger of evaluating, estimating, and judging every person we meet. And often enough we find ourselves on the verge of condemning and passing sentence on them. Silence prevents us from doing this. It keeps confronting us with ourselves. It prohibits us from taking the path to projecting our shadow side on others. The ancients were aware of the danger of constantly thinking and talking about others. It is reported of Father Agathon that he carried a stone in his mouth for three years until he learned to cope with silence and stop judging his brothers in his heart.

It often requires the conscious practice of silence so that the heart too can keep silent. We often have to expressly forbid ourselves to talk about others so that we can look on them without prejudice.

The early monks have often been criticized for the harshness of their asceticism. But the many admonishments not to judge and the beautiful stories of compassionate monks show us the opposite. In fact the monks saw not-judging as a criterion for the right way. Those who judge others haven't really learned to know themselves. Today there are many pious movements that live at the expense of other people. They wall themselves off while they drag others down and abuse them. Whenever people have to demonize those who follow a different spiritual path, it's a sign that there's something wrong with their path. Their demonizing points to the demon in their own heart that they refuse to acknowledge. They repress it and project it onto their neighbors. Those who have sincere self-knowledge will be spontaneously compassionate. They know deep in their hearts that basically we all need God's compassion. It's always a wonder of grace when God lets the good triumph in us.

But for the monks silence is still more than not-judging. Silence is *the* spiritual path pure and simple. In silence we encounter ourselves and our inner reality. But silence is also a way to become free from the thoughts that continuously occupy us. This is not an external silence, but a silence of the heart. Still, outer silence can help the heart to become quiet, the emotions to calm down and stop running our lives. Thus we are told of Father Moses, a former brigand, who was often insulted because of his black skin: "Another time there was an assembly in the skete, and the fathers wished to put him to the test and treated him as if he were nothing, saying: 'What is this Ethiopian doing among us?' He listened to them in silence. After the assembly broke up, they said to him: 'Father, didn't you get upset?' He answered: 'Yes, I did get upset, but I couldn't bring myself to speak'" (Ps. 77:4).

Father Moses was disturbed by the unfair words of the brothers. But he deliberately kept silence so that his emotions could calm down. He fought his agitation through silence. He didn't repress the injustice, but chose to heal the injury through silence. Speaking out about injuries is surely a good means to heal them. Modern psychotherapy has made that clear enough. But there is definitely another cure: silence. In silence the inner disturbances can quiet down, the dust cloud can settle, to let the heart clear up. It is like cloudy wine, which becomes clear after lying quietly in storage.

The second aspect of silence is letting go. In silence we let go of what constantly preoccupies us. We let go of our thoughts and our wishes. We let go of everything that would take control of us and that we feverishly cling to. So long as we cling to our success, our life makes no headway. So long as we cling to people, our relationships are troubled. Silence is the art of letting go in order to discover another foundation in oneself: God. Only when I have discovered my foundation in God can I let go of my profession, my role, my relationships, my possessions. Then I am no longer defining myself by the good will of others; my whole identity no longer hinges upon my success or my property. Letting go is the way to get in touch with my inner source, to discover the true wealth in my soul: God, who gives me everything that I need for life.

The monks practice silence not as an end in itself, but as a means to becoming one with God. Encountering oneself and letting go are the two necessary steps to oneness with God.

Silence is first of all the art of being entirely present, of giving oneself unreservedly to the moment. When random thoughts are forever rushing through our head, they keep us from being present, and we are always somewhere else. Being present is the necessary condition for being able to meet the God who is present. But the goal of silence is to become one with God, to be so open to God that he fills our thinking and feeling, that we sense him at the bottom of our heart, that we experience him as the source of our inner life, as the source that never dries up because it is divine.

Six

Analyzing Our Thoughts and Feelings

The encounter with oneself that the monks sought in silence and that they saw as a prerequisite for the encounter with God is for Evagrius Ponticus primarily a meeting with the thoughts and feelings in one's own heart. Among the desert fathers Evagrius is considered a specialist in dealing with thoughts and passions. He experienced them himself and wrote about them again and again in his books, to share his experience with others.

It was said of him: "If you wish to learn all the temptations that he experienced at the hands of the demons, then read the book that he wrote against the objections of the demons. There you will see all his power and his temptations. That is why he put them down in writing, so that those who read them may be strengthened and see that they aren't the only ones to be tempted in this way. He is the one who taught us which thoughts may be overcome in which way."

Evagrius comes to terms with the fact that a large part of our spiritual life consists in paying attention to our passions, in getting acquainted with them and dealing properly with them. The goal of this dealing is *apatheia,* a condition of inner quiet and serenity. In *apatheia* the passions are no longer in conflict with one another, but in accord. Evagrius also calls *apatheia* the health of the soul. The goal of the spiritual path is thus not a moral ideal of freedom from error, but the health of the soul. The soul is healthy, Evagrius says, when it is in harmony with itself and capable of love. Only those who achieve *apatheia* can really love. Indeed, *apatheia* actually *is* love.

Evagrius was a Greek, and hence he constructs the spiritual path in accordance with the Greek image of humanity. Greek philosophy was acquainted with three realms in the human person: the *desirous* part (*epithymia*), the *emotional* part (*thymos*), and the *intellectual* part (*nous*). These are also, by the way, the realms known to the enneagram, a system of self-knowledge that derives from Sufism and has close similarities with the nine *logismoi* (Greek for "reasonings" or "arguments") of Evagrius. The enneagram speaks of the gut type, the heart type, and the head type.

Evagrius then coordinates each of the three realms with three *logismoi,* which are emotionally accented thoughts that can rule a person; they are the passions of the soul, the drives that one must confront. In the negative sense Evagrius also calls the *logismoi* vices and relates them to demons that infect humans. Hence dealing with these thoughts and passions is at the same time a struggle with the demons. In this process the demons have more than just a negative meaning. They are also forces that humans can bend to their will. In Plato the "daimons" were thoroughly good energies, which

Persian dualism later turned into negative powers. For Evagrius they are forces of this world, personified psychological mechanisms at work in humans. The meaning of Evagrius for our time undoubtedly lies in his sharp-eyed account of "demonology" as a way of dealing with the passions and the laws of the human soul.

Evagrius challenges us to observe precisely our feelings and our thoughts, the demons and their laws: "If any should wish to know the evil demons from their own experience and become familiar with their art, I would advise them to carefully observe their thoughts. They should pay heed to the intensity and to the ebbing of their thoughts, when they arise and when they pass away. They should observe the variety of their thoughts, the regularity with which they recur, the demons responsible for them, which give way to succeeding ones, and which do not. Then they should beg Christ to explain to them everything that they have observed. For the demons are especially infuriated by those who are armed with such knowledge in their practice of virtue."

Evagrius's account of self-observation might almost be found in a psychology textbook explaining the various mechanisms of the soul and the connections of the individual feelings and emotions: "It is very important for us that we also learn to distinguish the various demons and to determine the attendant circumstances of their appearance. Our thoughts can teach us this. . . . Furthermore, we should note which demons attack less often and which are the more burdensome, which abandon the field more quickly and which put up stronger resistance. Finally we should also get to know the ones that attack immediately and seduce us into blasphemy. It is quite essential to know this exactly, so that when the various evil thoughts go to work in their characteristic fashion, we can oppose them with effective words, that is, words that correctly identify the one that is at work. We have to do that before they wrench us out of our frame of mind. Only in this way shall we, with God's grace, make good progress. We shall chase them off, but they will grow angry and at the same time wonder how we recognized them so acutely."

Precise knowledge about the emotions and passions is the prerequisite for dealing successfully with them. And the goal of our struggle is again *apatheia,* inner freedom. In psychological terms we can say that the goal is a mature handling of our emotions, a balanced relationship to our passions, reconciliation with ourselves and our shadow side, a wholeness in which the shadow is integrated and serves our spiritual efforts.

Evagrius sees in familiarity with the passions a fulfillment of the saying of Jesus about the cleverness of serpents: "Our Lord said, 'Be wise as serpents and innocent as doves' (Matt. 10:16). The monks must be in truth without guile and gentle, and let their disputes be in all gentleness, according to the word of the prophet. But let the eye of their spirit be agile, and let them be cunning in the arts of the demons, like the ichneumon [a species of Egyptian mongoose], which observes the tracks of the game, so that he can say, 'The thoughts of the Evil one are not hidden from us,' and, 'My eye looks upon my enemies, and my ears will hear of the evil ones who fight against me.' "

Thus, like the mongoose, we should study the tracks of the demons in order to catch them. The serpent is at once a symbol of the wisdom of nature and of sexuality. Acquiring the cleverness of serpents, therefore, also means being reconciled to our sexuality, becoming familiar with it, so as to integrate its wisdom and power into our spiritual path. The desert fathers made themselves familiar with negative thoughts and feelings. They had no fear of contact with the demons. For them that was a daily struggle, in which they acquired an increasingly exact knowledge of the opponent. Their writings speak of experience with the passions in our hearts and the powers in our unconscious.

1. Evagrius associates the vices of gluttony, unchastity, and greed with the *desirous* part. Eating, sexuality, and ownership are three basic drives in human beings that cannot be simply cut off and ignored. For in their role as basic instincts they urge us on to life, indeed, in the final analysis, to God. It all depends on how we deal with these drives, that is, whether we let ourselves be ruled by them, whether we become creatures of instinct or make positive use of their power and let ourselves be driven by them on the path to life and to God.

Evagrius describes the first instinct of gluttony, or gourmandise, not so much as excessive eating or a stuffing ourselves with negative feelings, but as fearful concern about one's heath, as fear of falling short, of not having enough food and medicine, or fear of getting sick because of asceticism. Eating is, of course, a basic human need, and one goal of eating is pleasure. Some people stuff themselves with food because they don't want to sense their anger. Food can also be a replacement for love. Many eaters devour everything in sight, but can't really enjoy anything. True asceticism consists in learning how to enjoy. Then the proper balance in eating will automatically assert itself, and the fear of running short will vanish. Unconsciously it is the fear of going hungry, in the literal and metaphorical senses.

Ultimately the goal of eating is to become one with God. That is why all religions have sacred meals. In the Eucharist it is precisely by eating bread that we become one with Christ, and through him, with God. Mystics have described unity with God as *fruitio Dei,* the enjoyment of God: eating as a basic act through which we are allowed to enjoy God.

Evagrius describes the second vice of lust as follows: "The demon of unchastity is concerned with greed for the body. Those who lead a life of abstinence find themselves more exposed to his assaults than others. For the demon would have them stop practicing this virtue. Anyway, so he would have them believe, it yields no profit. It is typical of this demon to play out before them impure actions, to dirty them, and finally to lead them astray into speaking and hearing words as if all that were taking place before their eyes."

Sexuality is a crucial force in human beings. It contains the longing for vitality, for self-transcendence, for ecstasy. Sex can be an important source of spirituality. Evagrius certainly doesn't deny that. But he sees the danger of taking refuge in a world of appearances. Sexuality has a great deal to do with frustration. Many people who can't endure disappointment take flight into sex. In that case it is not a place of intimate love and ecstasy, not union with the beloved, but fantasizing one's way into the illusory world of sexual satisfaction. Evagrius is speaking not of the union of man and woman in the sexual act, but of the flight into sexual fantasies. Here sexuality becomes an illusion. Instead of meeting a real person and giving oneself over wholly to that person, I use sex to represent to myself my own world, an illusory world where everything is wonderful. I don't have to have any consideration for anyone, but just live out my sexuality by myself.

This is a real danger, as indicated by the many reports today about sexual exploitation of children and sexual harassment of women in the workplace. Here sex is not being really lived; people shy away from taking the trouble to give themselves to the other and carefully achieving union with that person. Sex is seen as the satisfaction of lust, not as the expression of a love that feels its way into the heart of the other person. And so, with their non-integrated sexuality, people injure the dignity of others. There are hardly any more painful injuries than sexual injuries, hardly any more brutal and degrading forms of violence than sexual violence, when it lowers people to the level of a commodity.

In his description of unchastity Evagrius shows that he is in no way rejecting sexuality, a charge often made against the early monks. Instead he points to the fact that, just like eating, sex can be misused to flee from reality. Through the use of eating one stuffs one's anger and frustration. By using sex one can satisfy oneself, even if one is not content. And we can take refuge in it, if we do not trust ourselves to really meet another person and give ourselves to that person. In this case a faulty encounter, an inadequate readiness to love, is compensated with sex. In truth this harms the person, checks the process of becoming fully human, and perverts sex into a blockade of God, while an integrated sexuality worthy of human beings is always an expression of love for God.

Spirituality becomes alive only when sexuality is integrated into the religious path. When spirituality runs shallow, it bears witness to the fact that sex has not been contemplated and accepted. Evagrius doesn't want us to suppress sex, but to deal with it consciously. And without such conscious dealing with sex there is no human maturity and no real spirituality.

The third *logismos* of the instinctual desires, according to Evagrius, is greed. The striving for possessions is an essential part of human life, and it contains a longing for rest. Possessions lead us to expect that we will have no more cares and will be able to calmly spend our time living. But experience shows that possessions can possess *us,* that we are possessed by our striving for more and more things. Evagrius portrays the consequences of greed through some effective images. While the person with nothing is compared to a high-flying eagle, soaring freely in the air, unburdened by cares, he says of the rich: "But those who are very well off are shackled with cares and tied like a dog to a chain. Even when they are forced to emigrate, they bear the memory of their goods around with them like a heavy burden and a useless weight. They are tormented by sadness, and whenever they reflect, they are cruelly plagued. They leave their possessions behind and are tortured by grief. And even when death comes, they give up the present world with a pathetic lament. They surrender their souls and yet do not bid farewell to their possessions, which rather drag them along with them, since passion holds them down."

Our hunger for possessions is never satisfied if we direct it only to earthly things. However many things we own, this cannot quench our deepest longing for rest and contentment, for harmony with ourselves. Hence the New Testament transforms this desire by pointing us to an inner possession: to the pearl of great price, to the treasure buried in the field. We can find immeasurable riches in ourselves, in our soul, when we find God and all the possibilities God has given us. And when we turn toward this inner wealth, our striving for external possessions will not become immoderate.

Nowadays, of course, one sometimes sees the demonization of possessions and the ideological glorification of poverty, neither of which is especially helpful. Poverty is sometimes confused with an absence of culture. If poverty is only a negation of life, then it doesn't set us free. Genuine poverty deals humanely with the desire for possessions. It admits this striving, but it relativizes it, because it knows of a deeper wealth. Only for the sake of this inner value can we let go of external possessions, can we become increasingly free from greed.

2. Evagrius correlates the *emotional* realm of human beings to the three *logismoi* of sadness, of anger, and of acedia.

"*Sadness* can sometimes arise when a person's wishes go unfulfilled. Sometimes it also appears in the company of anger. If it arises as a consequence of needs and wishes that have not been met, it usually occurs in this way: such persons think first of all of their homes, of their parents, or of the life they led before. If they put up no resistance to this thought, or willingly go along with it or give into pleasures, even if only in their imagination, they are completely overcome. But in the end the thoughts they delighted in fade away, and they sink into melancholy. Their present circumstances prevent their thoughts from becoming reality. And so these unhappy persons are troubled insofar as they have abandoned themselves to such thoughts."

Evagrius distinguishes sadness (*lype*) from sorrow (*penthos*). While sorrow is an essential part of human maturation, as grief-work, as a processing of experiences of loss, sadness as self-pity is unfruitful. People take refuge in self-pity when their wishes are not fulfilled. Sadness often conceals exaggerated wishes of life. Because I am not the greatest, I don't even enter the struggle and take flight into sadness.

Sorrow can weep. Its tears can soften the hardened soul and make it fruitful. The tears of sorrow can be transformed into tears of joy. Sadness cannot weep; it is whiny; it bathes in its own self-pity. For Evagrius sadness consists above all in fruitless clinging to the past. One continually imagines the feelings one had before, back home with one's parents, the security, the freedom from cares, etc. Though it sometimes can be good to busy oneself with one's past, to assimilate it and sense in it the roots of the present, it doesn't get us very far when we are constantly looking into the past and longing for what it held. For Evagrius it's especially dangerous to flee from present reality into the past, which is gone once and for all and will never again be real. We can, certainly, learn a great deal for the present from the past. But when it turns into flight from the present, the past prevents us from facing today's tasks and coming to maturity by working on them.

Whiles in sadness we react passively to our unfulfilled wishes, *anger* is an active response. Evagrius also identifies anger with a demon. For him anger clearly shows how humans can be utterly dominated by another force.

"Anger is the most vehement of the passions. It is a welling up of the excitable part of the soul directed against someone who has injured us or by whom we believe ourselves injured. It unceasingly irritates our souls and forces its way into our awareness, especially during prayer time. In doing so, it makes the image of the person who has done us wrong rise up before us. Sometimes it goes on for a long time and is transformed into resentment, which causes bad experiences during the night. Generally this weakens the body. Insufficient nourishment is taken. Persons vexed by anger look pale and are increasingly troubled by images in dreams where they are attacked by wild, poisonous animals. Again and again they notice that these last four effects of resentment accompany their thoughts with particular frequency."

Evagrius does a precise analysis of anger, which is not simply aggression, because aggression can have a thoroughly positive meaning. Aggression aims to regulate the relationship between nearness and distance. Anger is uncontrolled aggression: the individual can no longer think clearly and is dominated by it. Anger prevents us from praying. Indeed it can lead to a loss of appetite and shape our dreams so that our consciousness becomes increasingly penetrated by negative feelings. Anger can make us sick. When in the grip of anger we have no distance from those who have injured us. It gives them so much power that they come after us everywhere. It invades our prayers, our mealtimes, our dreams. We are never free of it; it is like being possessed.

At one point Evagrius says that the demon of anger eats up the human soul. Nowadays this is confirmed by psychology, which has grounds for assuming that cancer often has a psychic cause. When one constantly thrusts something down, sooner or later the body reacts to this and is eaten up by it in the truest sense of the word.

The most dangerous demon is that of *acedia,* which inwardly tears the monk apart. Evagrius describes the effects of this demon as follows: "He begins his attack on the monk around the fourth hour and doesn't let up till about the eighth hour. At first it seems to the monk that the sun, if it is moving at all, moves very, very slowly, and that the day has been dragging on for at least fifty hours. He feels impelled to keep looking out the window, to leave the cell, to carefully check the sun in order to determine how far it still is from the ninth hour.... Slowly the demon makes hatred rise in the heart of the monk — hatred of the place where he finds himself, hatred of his present life, and of the work he is doing.... In other words the demon stops at nothing to get the monk to turn his back on his cell and give up the fight. But if this demon is conquered, another demon will not quickly replace him. A state of deep peace and inexpressible joy is the fruit of a victorious wrestling with him."

Acedia is the incapacity to be in the moment. Its victims have no desire to work and none to pray. They can't even enjoy doing nothing. They are always somewhere else with their thoughts. The inner unrest, the inability to enjoy the moment, disrupts them. Acedia is an expression of the flight from reality. Its victims don't wish to look their own reality in the eye. Their thoughts and actions are always somewhere else. They become incapable of doing anything consistent, of really committing themselves to anything or anyone.

Acedia is also called the noonday devil, because it makes its appearance at noon. But this can also be understood symbolically, and in that case acedia is primarily the demon of midlife. In midlife we no longer take pleasure in what we are used to doing. We wonder what's the point of it all. What we have hitherto achieved seems boring and empty. But we also fail to find anything to engage our interest. So we loll about, get cynical, and criticize everything. We feel no real desire for anything. The demon of midlife is a challenge to find a new orientation, to move from the outside to the inside and to discover new values in our soul that will give new meaning to the second half of life.

Nowadays acedia seems to be a basic attitude on the part of many young people too. They are incapable of committing themselves to anything, of being enthusiastic about anything. They can't live in the moment. They always have to be experiencing something new. For the violent among them brute force against others is the only way to feel alive. This makes it especially clear how destructive acedia can be. People incapable of living will live at others' expense; they will have to hit others to have any feeling themselves.

3. The three *logismoi* of the *intellectual* realm are the thirst for glory, envy, and pride (*hybris*).

Thirst for glory is constant boasting in the presence of others. One does everything purely to be seen by people. Evagrius puts it this way: "The thought of the thirst for glory is a truly difficult companion. He likes to come forth in persons who desire to live virtuously. He awakens a desire in them to tell others how hard their struggle is. In this fashion they seek honor from others. Such people like to fancy themselves, for example, curing women.... They imagine that men and women are knocking on their door, hoping to meet them and talk with them, forcing them to come along if they hesitate."

When I have a thirst for glory I am constantly thinking about others and their opinion of me. What effect am I having on them? Do they approve of what I do? I don't stand by myself; I make myself dependent on the judgment of others. Indeed, I am forever thinking up ways of making my next appearance on the stage as effective as possible so that I may get properly applauded.

Naturally it does all of us good to be acknowledged and confirmed. And it would be hypocritical to think that we are completely untouched by recognition and praise. The thirst for recognition creeps into everything, even our most pious actions. The point is not to become entirely free of it, but to relativize the thirst for recognition, so as not to make ourselves dependent upon it.

We ourselves sense how painful it is, for example, when sixty- and seventy-year-olds are still wholly focused on what others think and expect. That isn't life, but having our lives lived for us by somebody else.

Envy makes its appearance in continuous comparisons with others. I can't meet another person without comparing myself with that person. I immediately begin to appraise people, to value, devalue, and revalue them. I look for their weak points or downgrade their performance as inhibited or morbid, their success as illusory, their intelligence as weak, etc. And conversely, when I don't succeed at this, I devalue myself and put others on a pedestal.

In envy too I am not standing by myself, I am not content with myself, I have no sense of dignity. I recognize my value only by comparison with others. This is very exhausting. It either forces me to surpass others or plunges me into depression because I see no chance of holding my own with others.

Hybris, or pride, blinds people. Proud persons have so identified with their ideal image that they refuse to look at their reality. "The demon of pride is the cause of the worst fall a person can have. For pride seduces people into seeking the cause of their virtuous actions not in God but in themselves.... In the end the proud come down with the worst possible sickness; they become mentally deranged, succumb to madness, and fall prey to hallucinations that make them see whole hosts of demons in the skies."

In *hybris* people exalt themselves so far into the fantastic world of their own ideals that they lose touch with reality. This makes them delusional. C. G. Jung calls this attitude inflation: we pump ourselves up with ideals and notions that we aren't entitled to. Inflation always occurs when we identify ourselves with an archetypal image, for example, of the prophet: "I am the only one who can see through it all, who dares to say the truth." Or with the image of martyr: "No one understands me; I just have to suffer, because, like Jesus, I'm so different, because I alone stand up for the truth." Such words often have a pious ring to them. But behind them is *hybris,* wanting to be like God or like people whom God has given a special call.

Indeed, this sort of *hybris* blinds us. As a prophet I'm blind to my own reality. I tell the world what's right, but I don't know myself at all. I refuse to look at myself. Jesus heals the man born blind by spitting on the ground and lovingly rubbing the clay into his eyes, as if to say: "You too, after all, have been taken from the earth. Reconcile yourself with the dirt that's in you, with your shadow side. Be a human being, and then you can see again. As long as you deny your earthliness, you won't be able to see."

Dealing with Our Passions

In reading the description of these nine *logismoi* we sense how much psychological experience Evagrius gathered in his *kellion*. But he thought there was something still more important than knowing about the *logismoi:* handling thoughts and feelings. Evagrius advises a different method for every passion. The three basic drives — eating, sex, and greed — are transformed through fasting, asceticism, and almsgiving. Here discipline is a good way not to suppress the drives, but to shape them, so that they can serve us as a power source. We overcome sadness by fleeing dependency on the world, by letting go of what we are clinging to, and by setting ourselves free.

Most of the advice Evagrius gives is about dealing with anger. Irritation, anger, and resentment keep us continuously occupied in everyday life.

One helpful suggestion is, before going to sleep, to look at our annoyances and lay them aside, so that they don't become lodged in our unconscious during dreams and then express themselves the next day in a diffuse discontent. When we take our irritations with us into the night, we lose control over ourselves; we continue to be driven by the anger and resentment in our unconscious.

"Don't let the sun go down on your anger, otherwise while you rest at night the demons will come and make you anxious, rendering you all the more cowardly for the next day's battle. For the delusions of the night usually arise through the exciting influence of anger. And nothing makes people so ready to give up their struggle as when they cannot control its stirrings."

When anger has infected our unconscious, we lose all control over ourselves, and we are at the mercy of our anger. But that tears us apart. Thus, the notion of looking over our anger once more and laying it aside in prayer to God is not primarily a moral demand, but a psychological imperative that serves the health of body and soul.

At conferences of priests one often hears complaints that in the evening they come back from some sessions frustrated and angry, and then they can find no pleasure in meditation or reading. Instead they stuff their frustration with food, drink, and TV. But then the unassimilated feelings collect in them and come out the next day in a vague sense of discontent and emptiness. Distancing ourselves from our negative feelings through prayer in the evening opens us up in our dreams to God's healing comfort.

Above all Evagrius warns against playing mind games with anger: "And do not abandon yourself to anger in such a way that you dispute in your thoughts with the one who has vexed you." For that casts a dark shadow over our soul and disturbs our mind. But we may also use anger as a positive force, by turning it against the demons, temptations, and thoughts that hold us back from life: "We may be angry if we turn against the demons and if we do battle with pleasures."

Rage is often an important force that liberates us from negative memories and drives from our mind the people who have injured us. So long as we circle round the injury, we give power over us to those who have wounded us. Some people wallow continually in their own wounds. Rage, then, is a very important force. If I can feel rage toward those who have injured me, I can distance myself, I can draw a line between other people's problems and my own. Rage is the first step to freedom and healing.

I have observed several times how women who were sexually abused as children still feel guilty but detect no rage at all. Only when they get in touch with their rage can they work out their traumatic experience. Rage is the power to distance ourselves from traumatic experience and to get rid of those who have injured us so that we can be free again, so that God's healing spirit can once again penetrate us.

With regard to *acedia* Evagrius gives two pieces of advice. One concerns steadfastness. We are to make up our minds and stay in our cell, simply enduring whatever is going on within us: "Just accept what the temptation brings on you. Above all, look this temptation of acedia in the eye, for it is the worst of all. But it also leads to the greatest purification of the soul. To flee or avoid such conflicts makes the spirit clumsy, cowardly, and fearful."

When I endure my inner unrest and take a closer look at it, then perhaps I can discover what is stirring in it. Then I sense that it has a meaning. Unrest might free me from the illusion of being able to better myself through discipline and taking myself in hand. Unrest shows me how powerless I am. When I become reconciled with it, this cleanses the soul and gives new inner clarity. Amid my unrest I sense a deep peace. So the unrest is allowed to be. In the end it is designed to prod me on to God: Augustine found that restlessness prompted him to find rest in God.

The second counsel relates to prayer: "When we are tempted by acedia, it is good, amid the tears of our soul, to divide it, so to speak, into two parts: into one part that encourages and another that is encouraged. We sow seeds of an unshakable hope in ourselves when we sing with King David: 'Why are you cast down, O my soul, and why are you disquieted within me? Hope in God for I shall again praise him, my help and redeemer, to whom I look'" (Ps. 42:5).

What Evagrius is recommending here is the "antirrhetic method" (that is, flowing in the opposite direction), which he elaborates primarily in his book *Antirrhetikon*. There it is not just a help in times of acedia but in all situations. In the face of every thought that might make us sick, that bars the way to freedom, love, and life, Evagrius collects a saying from the Bible to oppose it. Thus, persons who constantly reproach themselves for the sins of their youth and tell themselves that everything has gone wrong with them should continually recite 2 Corinthians 5:17: "If any one is in Christ, he is a new creation; the old has passed away, behold, the new has come." Such a saying gradually transforms our feelings of sadness and self-pity. It brings us into contact with the positive force in us, with the Holy Spirit, who is already at work in us, who pours forth like a wellspring, ready to let us draw from it.

To remedy the *thirst for glory* Evagrius advises the use of memory. We should remind ourselves where we come from, what passions we had to struggle with, and how it wasn't thanks to our own merit that we conquered, but to Christ who protected us. Memory will show us that we have no guarantee for success in life, only God's grace. Evagrius says that the demon of pride and vaingloriousness will continually arise in us precisely when we have made progress in asceticism.

The most effective remedy is contemplation. When we have become one with God through contemplation, then it no longer makes any difference what people think of us. Then we no longer define ourselves by the recognition and confirmation we get; we have reached our foundation in God.

Evagrius's most systematic presentation tells us how to deal with our thoughts and feelings. But this topic also keeps recurring in the sayings of the fathers, who offer many other counsels about reacting to the passions. The fathers continually advise us to make ourselves familiar with the passions. Dialogue with them can show us the positive energy contained in them and how this force could be integrated into our life. Two sayings from Poimen make this point:

"A brother came to Father Poimen and said: 'Father, I have all sort of thoughts, and because of them I am in peril.' Poimen led him outdoors and told him: 'Spread out your shirt and stop the winds with it!' He answered:

'I can't do that!' Then the old man said: 'If you can't do that, neither can you prevent your thoughts from coming to you. Your responsibility is to resist them." As this saying makes clear, we cannot hold off our thoughts. We aren't responsible for the thoughts that pop up in our heads, only for the way we handle them. So we are not bad when thoughts press us hard. *We* aren't thinking these thoughts; they come to us from the outside. This distinction between ourselves as persons and the thoughts that flow into us is crucial in enabling us to deal properly with our thoughts. It will prevent us from instantly accusing ourselves when hatred or jealousy, say, enter our minds. Rather we will consider how to react to them and not let them dominate us. The point is not to repress them, but to talk to them, as the second saying shows:

"Father Poimen once asked Father Joseph: 'What should I do when the passions come upon me? Should I resist them or let them come in?' The old man said: 'Let them in and fight with them.' When he got back to the skete, he sat down. And one of the Thebans came to the skete and told the brothers: 'I asked Father Joseph: When the passions come near me, should I resist them or let them in? And he said to me: Don't let them in at all; clear them away on the spot!' Father Poimen heard that Father Joseph had spoken thus to the Thebans. He got up and went to Panepho to see him and said: 'Father, I entrusted my thoughts to you, and, look, you spoke one way to me and another to the Thebans.' The old man replied: 'Don't you know that I love you?' He said, 'Yes!' And the old man: 'Didn't you say to me: Speak to me as if to yourself?' He answered: 'That's right!' Then the old man said: 'When the passions come and you engage in give-and-take with them, they will make you more tried and tested. I spoke to you as if to myself. But there are others for whom the coming of the passions is of no profit. They need to cut them off on the spot."

Clearly there are two different ways of dealing with the passions. One way is to become familiar with them, to let them enter so as to observe them more carefully. By getting to know the passions I can discover the energy within me. And perhaps the passion can tell me what kind of longing is dwelling within it, where it actually wants to take me. Dialogue with the passions shows me what cannot live in me. For example, if there is great rage in me, this always has some meaning. It makes no sense simply to crush it. Perhaps it shows me that I have given others too much power. Rage might give me the strength to eject the other from myself, to liberate myself from them.

A woman whose husband was an alcoholic had feelings of hatred toward him; she even thought of killing him. She accused herself of being thoroughly evil for even thinking such things. This happens to many people who blame themselves for their negative thoughts. The monks are more compassionate on this score. They say that the thought isn't evil; it has a meaning. I just have to find the strength that lies within it. In the woman's feeling of hatred for her husband lies an impulse that's saying: "I have a right to love too. I'm not going to let myself be done in." If I live out this impulse, I don't need the hatred. The feeling of hate that comes to the surface in me is not bad. It's an alarm bell to signal that I'm giving others too much power over myself. If I hear it and act accordingly, the feeling will retreat. If I repress the feeling, I'll never get rid of the hatred. And then it will destroy me. Thus, we aren't responsible for the thoughts that turn up in our heads, but for how we deal with them.

Still — as Father Joseph tells us — there are people for whom it's better simply to cut off negative thoughts and feelings, not to let them approach us. If I notice that I keep thinking about people who have hurt me, then it might be useful to forbid myself these thoughts. I can really think these thoughts through and reflect on how I should react to them; I can work through them and put them aside. But if despite all this they keep coming back, it makes no sense to go on chewing them over. Then I simply have to cut them off and throw them out. Other people are fascinated by the thoughts of suicide that they conjure up. Here one has to get rid of such thoughts whenever they occur. Spending too much time on them can be dangerous. There are some destructive thoughts that we have long since seen through, but that nonetheless keep surfacing. Here too it makes no sense to go on analyzing them. One simply has to bid them farewell.

I have to find out for myself which method I should use. Normally the appropriate thing is to think through a feeling. In this case I often need the help of another person with whom I can talk about my feelings. But when the thoughts nevertheless keep returning, it can be helpful to close the door on them. Then again there are people who ban negative thoughts a priori, and who for that very reason are all the more tormented by them.

Here the appropriate choice would be to do a more careful study of them.

A young wife and mother told me that she is often horrified by the thought that she might murder her child. Sometimes when she is changing her baby's diaper, the thought comes to her out of the blue that now she could kill the baby. Then she has a panic attack that this might actually happen. Here it makes no sense to forbid the thought, because then it will only land on her with a vengeance. If she were to speak with this thought, it would probably tell her that she should make peace with her aggression. As a mother, she believes that she can only love her child, that she is not allowed to have any negative thoughts. But it's quite natural for a mother to feel not just love, but aggression too. The meaning of this aggression is that she has not totally identified with the child, but is seeking the necessary distance to be able to love the child over the long haul. Thus the mother would have to listen to her aggressions and then dissociate herself from them and take better care of herself. But if she buries all her aggressive feelings, these uncontrolled thoughts about killing her child will come back.

Dialogue with one's thoughts is called for above all in the case of *fear.* Fear has a meaning too; it's trying to tell me something. Without fear I would have no measuring rod; I would constantly make too many demands on myself. But fear often blocks me. So when I talk to my fear, it can direct me to the presence of a false outlook on life. Fear often originates in an ideal of perfection. I'm afraid of disgracing myself, of making a mistake. I don't trust myself to speak in a group for fear of stuttering, or anxiety that the others might not like what I say. I'm afraid of reading out loud, because I might get stuck. In this case fear always points to exaggerated expectations.

In the final analysis it's pride that causes fear. Thus the conversation with my fear could lead to humility. I could reconcile myself to my limits, to my weaknesses and mistakes. "I am allowed to make a fool of myself. I don't have to be able to do everything."

But there are also fears that do not point to any false outlook on life, but are necessarily bound up with being human. For example, there is the fear of loneliness, the fear of loss, the fear of dying. In every person fear of death is always present, but in some people it reaches menacingly high levels. So it's important to speak to your fear. "Yes, in any event I *will* die." Fear can help me to reconcile myself with death, to come to an understanding with the fact that I am mortal. When I get to the bottom of my fear, when I let it in, I may sense in the middle of it a deep peace. Fear is transformed into serenity, freedom, and peace.

Another kind of fear can grip us when we take a look at our profession, our illness, our marriage. We worry whether we can make it in our marriage, whether we can be faithful, whether we can endure the pain of our illness. Nowadays one hears about the fear of commitment on the part of young people who don't want to tie themselves down forever, either to marriage or religious life. Here one of the sayings of the fathers shows us a different way to deal with this fear: "The story was told of Father Theodore and Father Lukios from Ennatu that for fifty years they ridiculed their own thoughts by saying: Once this winter is over, we're leaving. Then when summer came they would say: After this summer, we're heading off. These unforgettable fathers were forever doing that."

Many people feel anxiety when they imagine always being trapped in the same place, always teaching at the same school, always being tied down to this family. It can help to really say yes to my situation. But sometimes an absolute yes overburdens us; it heightens our fear that we may not be up to it. In that case the point might be to agree with the fathers from Ennatu that saying yes to today is enough. Tomorrow we may be somewhere else.

These methods have been taken over by many self-help groups. Members of Alcoholics Anonymous know they can't guarantee that they'll stay sober forever. They pray God for the strength to live without alcohol for just one day. The other thought — to leave the monastery or the marriage, to start drinking again — isn't totally denied. In fact one plays with it, but in so doing one takes away its power. The thought will come to us one way or another. So it makes no sense to declare outright war on it. If we deal playfully with it, the thought will never overpower us. The method of the fathers protects us from facing all the consequences at once. We enter upon a path in the hope that God is leading us. We can see the next stretch of road, but we don't think about the whole long, tedious way.

Another method of dealing with our thoughts and feelings, our passions and needs, consists in thinking them all the way through to the end, in picturing to ourselves all the consequences of admitting the passions into the imagination. In this way we can also discover which way the passions actually want to lead us. Sexual fantasies, for example, stand for something quite different, for the longing to be free, to let oneself fall, to be able to surrender. If I constantly wage war on my sexual fantasies and repress them, they will keep returning. When I think and feel them to the end, they can metamorphose into a drive for life, into an impetus toward God.

It is reported of Father Olympios that he allowed the thought of taking a wife to enter his mind, down to the least details. Indeed, he made a woman out of clay, looked at her, and said: "Look, that's your wife. Now you have to work to feed her. And he worked with great effort. After a day he again shaped clay and made a daughter out of it, and he told himself: your wife has had a child! Now you have to work even harder to feed and clothe your child. In so doing he worked himself to the bone, and so he told himself: if you can't bear all this labor, then don't go longing for a wife. God saw his exertion and took away the struggle from him, and he found rest." Father Olympios allowed room for the wish to sleep with a woman. Indeed he made himself one out of clay. He looked straight at his desire. But he also confronted the desire with reality. Living with a woman would mean working for her. Perhaps the argument strikes us as somewhat simplistic: not wanting a wife just because of all the work. But the decisive feature here is that, on the one hand, Olympios handles his need for a woman without anxiety: he not only imagines her; he forms a woman out of clay and really looks at her. But, on the other hand, he doesn't stop with the beautiful fantasy of living and sleeping with the woman: he envisions the consequences. He measures his desire against reality. And because his wish is thought out all the way into sober reality, it loses its threatening quality. Now he can deal soberly with his desire.

The problem of men and women celibates is that they get romantic notions of marriage. The question of whether they should marry or not can't be decided by some romantic idea, but by the sober question: is this really my path? I can find out whether it is or isn't by looking at the consequences. But this method doesn't apply just to celibates. Many people dream their way into castles in the air. They become restless because imagination promises them a far more beautiful world than the one they have. Here Olympios's method helps them to bring those castles down to earth, to confront fantasy with reality, to imagine it with all its consequences. Then it becomes transformed; it shows me what really wants to live in me and how I can connect this wish with reality, without simply chucking my previous life plans.

Another thought may press us hard: getting out of our former life, our former profession, and doing something completely different. Often all the arguments are useless here. The thought just keeps coming back. Here too some of the sayings of the fathers show us a way. A father who had struggled for years against the thought of visiting a certain confrère concretely imagined going to him, greeting him, and speaking to him. He imagined the meal with him, cooking something, having a good deal to eat and drink, "and immediately the struggle disappeared."

88

Some people who are dissatisfied with their way of life have to get down, busy themselves with their dream and test it, in order to be cured and turn to their old one with new energy and contentment. A married man who has fallen in love with another woman can often get free of his romantic dreams only by concretely imagining what it would be like to live with this woman, to give up everything he has known before, and to be with her day after day. If he measures his dream against reality, if he actually lets it in, he can take his leave of it.

With the antirrhetic method, which we have already seen in the overcoming of acedia, the point is likewise to get to know one's own thoughts and then to search the Scriptures for a healing text. This method of using a biblical passage to counter negative thoughts or feelings has been taken over by the American approach of so-called positive thinking. But there it often looks as if we are just manipulating our emotions, as if we just need to think positively and then everything will be all right.

Evagrius validates the antirrhetic method with the practice of both David and Jesus. Thus he writes in a letter that the intellect must first come to know the deceptive machinations of the demon. This is the prerequisite for the knowledge of Christ and for contemplation. The path in that direction passes through the struggle with the demons: "Hence it [the intellect] must fearlessly confront its enemy, as the blessed David shows, when he quotes voices as if they were coming from the mouth of the demons and then contradicts them. For when the demons say, 'When will he die and his name pass away?' then he says, 'I shall not die but live and proclaim the works of the Lord' (Ps. 118:17). And again when the demons say, 'Flee and dwell on the mountains like the sparrow' (Ps. 11:1), then he says, 'For he is my God and my Savior, my strong place of refuge; I shall not waver.' Thus, listen to the contradictory voices and love the victory, imitate David and pay heed to yourself!"

David's method consists in dividing his soul into two parts, one that is sad and one that encourages, one that is sick and one that is healthy. And then these two domains are supposed to engage in conversation. The sick part expresses itself in negative protests, such as: "I can't do it; nobody likes me; nobody cares about me; everything's going wrong with me." To fight off such thoughts one should look for a saying from Scripture, which is what Evagrius did for his brothers in his *Antirrhetikon:* "But because we don't quickly come up with the words that must be spoken against our enemies, the odious demons, because those words are scattered throughout the Scriptures and it is hard to find them, we have zealously collected the sayings from Scripture, so that, armed with them, we may powerfully track down the Philistines, while standing in the battle as strong men and soldiers of our victorious king Christ."

In this battle Christ himself is the model. When he was tempted by the devil, he quoted words from Scripture against Satan's lying proposals: "Our Lord Jesus Christ himself, who gave up everything to redeem us, has lent us the power to tread upon snakes and scorpions, and every power of the Evil one. And together with his whole teaching he handed down to us what he himself did when he was tempted by Satan, so that in the time of struggle, when the demons fight against us and hurl their missiles at us, we may contradict them by means of the Holy Scriptures, lest the infamous thoughts remain in us and subjugate our soul by the sin that is actually committed, staining it and plunging it into the death of sin.... For whenever the soul has no fitting thought available, to quickly and effortlessly contradict the Evil one, sin gets the upper hand."

The antirrhetic method requires that we first observe our thoughts precisely, that we note whether they make us sick or healthy, whether they lift us up or drag us down, whether they correspond to the Spirit of God. Evagrius describes the process of testing thoughts with the image of the gatekeeper: "Be a gatekeeper of your heart and let no thought in without questioning it. Examine every single thought one by one and ask it: 'Are you one of ours or one of our enemies?' And if he belongs to the house, he will fill you with peace. But if he belongs to the enemy, he will confuse you with anger or excite you with desire. Such are the thoughts of the demons." Here Evagrius is interpreting Jesus' parable of the doorkeeper (Mark 13:34–35). We should closely watch whatever thoughts are seeking entrance into our house. We should bar the door to the thoughts of the demons, which make us sick, which prevent us from living and close us off from God. We should lock them out with a verse of Scripture. And when we come upon these negative thoughts in our house, we should drive them out again with the help of a biblical text.

Even this method requires thorough self-exploration in advance, but its reaction to the thoughts is different. Here we don't engage in any dialogue with them. We don't ask what they wish to say to us, what power they contain; instead we oppose them with something. This method is always the right one when we sense that the thoughts are useless, that they aren't leading us on the path to life but only want to stop us from getting there. Above all this is an appropriate path to take when the thoughts keep recurring, when they have turned into a sort of script for life, as described by transactional analysis. This psychological school believes that many people are just living out their script in life. One young woman learned from therapy that her life script was, "All men are murderers." Obviously there is no way to live well with this sort of script. Another typical script says, "I am a failure, a loser, things always go wrong with me; I'll never blossom."

One can't just go on analyzing such lines. Examining these thoughts *can* explain where they came from, for example, that we got such messages from our parents. But knowing how they came about doesn't dissolve the thoughts. Here it helps to join Evagrius in a search through Scripture for lines that disarm and dispel such negative life scripts.

C. J. Jung believes that we have two poles in us: fear and trust, aggression and love, weakness and power. But we often get fixated on one pole, for example, on fear. In that case fear continually expresses itself in thoughts such as, "I can't do it. I'm afraid. What do others think about me? I'm making a fool of myself."

I can interrogate this fear, and ask what it wants to tell me. But I can also direct a verse at it from Psalm 118: "With the Lord on my side I do not fear. What can man do to me?" (v. 6). This won't simply drive away the fear. But it can get me into contact with the trust that is likewise hidden within me: I don't simply have fear within me, but trust as well. Thus the biblical text gets me in touch with what is already in me. And in this way the trust that is in me can become conscious and grow. This in turn will relativize my fear. Thus the antirrhetic method brings me into equilibrium. It fights back against negative thoughts and stops them from solidifying and controlling me.

Another method of dealing with my thoughts is to discuss them with someone else. Today the waiting rooms of psychologists are packed, because we don't dare to speak openly about ourselves in front of our friends. Above all we avoid discussing our negative feelings, our passions, our weaknesses, and our guilt. As a result many people remain alone with their thoughts; they repress them. But then the thoughts begin to boil up, until sooner or later the lid blows off. Talking about thoughts, the monks tell us, takes away the dangerous and destructive element in them. One monk says: "If you are hard pressed by impure thoughts, don't hide them; reveal them at once to your spiritual father, and destroy them. For insofar as one conceals his thoughts, they increase and grow stronger. Just like a snake that escapes from its hiding place and slithers away, the thought disappears the moment it is exposed. And as a worm eats away wood, evil thoughts destroy the heart. Those who reveal their thoughts are healed immediately; but those who hide them become sick from pride." The evil thought is compared to a worm that gnaws at the heart. If we lure the worm out in conversation, the wood will stay healthy, and the heart can breathe again.

EIGHT

Shaping Life Spiritually

It is important to the monks to provide a concrete structure for their day and their spiritual exercises. At first glance that seems to be a superficial matter. In reality it decides whether life is going to succeed or not. A healthy spirituality needs a healthy way of life.

"Father Poimen used to say, 'We found three bodily experiences with Father Pambo: daily fasting till evening, silence, and a great deal of manual labor.'" With these exercises Pambo reached spiritual maturity. Perseverance in these three things transformed him. In a similar way Anthony learned from an angel how his life could succeed. When he morosely asked the angel what he should do, he saw someone like himself: "He sat there and worked, then got up from his work, wove a rope, then got up again to pray. And behold, it was an angel of the Lord, who had been sent to give Anthony instruction and safety. And he heard the angel say: 'Act this way, and you will win salvation.' When he heard that, he was filled with great joy and courage, and by doing this he found redemption." The clear organization of the day, the healthy combination of prayer and work, of sitting and standing up, of weaving ropes and praying, is the path to inner peace. It clarifies negative feelings and establishes order in the person.

Father John is reported to have engaged in another practice: "It is said that when he came home from harvesting or from a get-together with the elders, he first took time for prayer, meditation, and psalm-singing, until his thoughts were restored to an orderly state." John doesn't simply allow free range to the emotions that have been stirred up by conversation with his brothers. First he takes time for prayer, so that his emotions can settle. When we bring home unsettled emotions and stuff them with lots of activity (of whatever kind), then they take root in the unconscious, and from there they spread a feeling of discontent. Just as our external life should be put in order, so should our thought processes. Disorganized thinking, the fathers tell us, gets the monks into a muddle and deliver them up to their passions. Those who give free rein to their thoughts and feelings without confronting them will be inwardly infected by them. Without noticing it, they will be driven by unconscious impulses and lose their freedom.

A similar story is told of John: "Once when he was on his way to the church in the skete and heard some brothers disputing there, he returned to his *kellion*. He walked around it three times, and only then did he go in. A few brothers who saw that, but couldn't imagine why he was doing it, came to him and asked him. But he answered: 'My ears were full of the wrangles, so I walked about to cleanse them, so that I could enter my *kellion* in peace.'" Here John does *not* take his thoughts home to quiet them down. Rather he frees himself from them even before he goes in. Walking is for him a way to shake off the negative emotions he met with among the disputing brothers.

Every evening numerous dramas are played out as husbands and wives come home from work, bringing with them a chaotic mass of negative feelings from the office. They are glad to see each other, but they are full of thoughts from work. And thus there is no meeting of minds; people talk past each other and unload problems dragged in from elsewhere. Here it would be a good exercise to take the path home more carefully, to leave time to consciously free oneself from the emotions of the workplace. Then we can openly encounter the family waiting for us. Then we will be alert and awake to whatever is on their mind.

Anthony is the source of the saying: "If possible the monk should confidently tell the elders how many steps he takes, or how much water he drinks in his cell, to be sure that he is not sinning." The external shaping of life is very important for the monks. They can tell from that whether they are healthy or not, whether they are really seeking God or only themselves. External order brings the monks internal order. It purifies their thinking and feelings; it creates space in which to become internally clear and transparent.

The spirituality of the early monks had the power to work out their lives to the last detail. Nowadays we are in danger of only writing *about* spirituality. But it doesn't appear in concrete life; it has no power to shape our lives. One evening I was staying at a rectory where during the meal the priest found nothing better to do than to turn on the TV. I thought to myself, he can preach all he wants tomorrow morning. If your life doesn't add up, then the sermon doesn't add up either; in that case spirituality is worthless.

The spirituality of the monks created a culture of life. It challenges us today to penetrate our lives with the spirit, to develop a spiritual culture of life that is also visible from the outside.

For the monks the path to a spiritual culture of life was always concrete practice. Generally there were three counsels that an elder would give a young monk when asked about the way to true monasticism.

"A man who lived together with other brothers, asked Father Bessarion: 'What should I do?' The old man answered him: 'Be silent and don't measure yourself against others.'" Silence and giving up comparisons were to be sufficient exercises for the monks. If they consistently stuck with it, they would purify their thinking and feeling; they would be open to God.

Anthony shows us other exercises: "Father Pambo asked Father Anthony: 'What should I do?' The old man answered: 'Don't count on your own righteousness, and don't regret something that is past, and practice restraint of the tongue and the belly.'" Once again Anthony is assigning quite concrete exercises. He doesn't assign some complex construct of ideas; he sends him off to perform practical life tasks that will become habitual for him, will lead him into the mystery of God and the mystery of humanity.

Along with continence of the tongue and belly, along with silence and fasting, humility is also described in many other sayings of the fathers as the royal road to God. For the monks humility is considered "the greatest virtue, for it lets a person rise up from the abyss, even when the sinner is like a demon."

The third practice consists in the interesting advice not to be sorry for something that is past. In my classes on confession I always stress the importance of repentance for sin. Only those who repent can find forgiveness. This is surely correct. But sometimes we think that we please God by being as contrite as possible, by running ourselves down and accusing ourselves. Here Anthony has different advice: what is over is over. This applies to past events; we shouldn't be forever ruminating over our past. But it also refers to our mistakes and sins. We shouldn't mourn for them either; they are over. We should not pay more attention to ourselves and our failures than to God: "For God is greater than our hearts, and he knows everything" (1 John 3:20). God knows about our failures. And we will sin again; we can't put up any guarantee for ourselves. But we should give sin no power over us. One way to deprive sin of such power is to let the past be, to give up thinking about it. We hold it out to God and pass it on to God. But then it's over and done with; we shouldn't worry about it anymore.

This advice from Anthony expresses great confidence in the grace and compassion of God, who knows and understands our heart.

Father Paul of Galatia says of himself and his daily exercises: "I always have these three things in mind: silence, mental humility, and telling myself that I have no cares." Once again we find the monks advising silence and humility as the basic attitude of the religious person. One father could even say: "Where humility is missing, God is missing too." Humility is the necessary prelude to experiencing God. Without humility we are in danger of pocketing God for our own purposes, of subordinating God to our thoughts and desires.

The third exercise consists in freedom from care. The monk practices this by always telling himself: "I have no cares." Evidently he has to keep prompting himself with this line, because thoughts of care *will* come up. No human being, of course, is exempt from care. Indeed, Martin Heidegger thought that care is the most basic feature of human existence. A person is essentially someone who cares (or worries). Still, by aiming the phrase, "I have no cares" at this care, the feeling can change, and I can find my trust in God's nearness growing. And so we have a way pointed out to us for practicing our trust in God. I'm not artificially talking myself into anything here; I'm not manipulating my ideas; I'm taking into account the fact that I have cares. But I try to practice concretely the biblical message of trust in God, who takes care of us, by continuously telling myself, "I have no cares."

The monks have always practiced what many psychologists today talk about (for example in autogenous training), namely, finding comfort through expressions of trust.

For the early monks spiritual life also meant the art of healthy living. It was no accident that so many of the monks got to be very old. Their asceticism didn't deny life, it promoted it. For their spiritual life the monks

adopted dietetics, the art of healthy living, which was
the most important task of ancient medicine. They understood the spiritual path as the art of healthy living. There
is no healthy life without a healthy lifestyle. Hence the
monks ordered their lives so clearly and recommended
a healthy succession of prayer and work, a combination
of waking and sleeping, eating and fasting, isolation and
togetherness as the guiding principle of a healthy life.
Through external order a person finds internal order.
Naturally, this is not a compulsory regimen one subjects oneself to, but a lifestyle that keeps body and soul
healthy. This lifestyle involves the budgeting of time,
food, work, housing, and a clear relationship to an elder.

Nowadays we could surely never imitate the lifestyle
of the old monks. But the basic principle that order outside leads us to order inside, that a healthy way of living
also makes the soul healthy, is something we can still
live today.

In the history of monasticism it is above all Benedict
who described a healthy way of life. For him the clear
structuring of life, of work, of community, and of power
was crucial for the recovery and maintenance of human
health. And although Benedict intended his Rule only for
a small community, it became a regulating factor for all
of Europe. From the small communities that lived according to this Rule there arose a source of culture for
the entire Western world. Culture is structured life. If I
shape my own life, if I give it a form that suits me and
does me good, then I will take pleasure in life. I have
the feeling that I am alive, not that my living is being
done for me. My style can be seen in the way I get up

in the morning, the way I begin my day, go to work, arrange my mealtimes, and end the day. A healthy lifestyle requires healthy rituals. When we don't pay attention to healthy rituals, unhealthy rituals creep in that involuntarily make us sick — for example, starting our day with a mad rush, wolfing down breakfast, always arriving late, etc. Healthy rituals put order in my life, and they give me the joy of shaping my life my own way.

Erhart Kästner speaks about the rites he observed on Mount Athos: "Alongside the urge to conquer the world, there lies an innate urge to keep stamping the same thing out of primordial forms. The soul feels good in rites. They are its solid shell. Here one can live... here stand the filled bowls, the sacrificial vessels of the soul. Here it goes out and goes in; the accustomed gifts, the accustomed meal. The head wants novelty; the heart always wants the same thing" (Kästner, 65).

Healthy rituals give life familiarity, security, clarity. Here we can live, here we can be at home.

NINE

Keeping Death before Our Eyes Every Day

In his Rule St. Benedict advises the monks to keep death before their eyes every day. In saying this, he summarizes what we are told in numerous stories about the monks: they lived in the awareness of their death. This makes them inwardly more vital and focused. Thinking about death liberated them from all fear. Thus a young monk asks an elder: "Why am I seized by fear when I go out at night?" The old man says: "Because the life of this world is still of value to you." Thinking about death removes our fear because we stop clinging to the world, to our health, to our life. And thinking about death enables us to live every moment consciously, to sense what the gift of life is, and to enjoy it every day.

In some sayings we feel the monks' deep longing for death. But this longing to die, to be with the Lord, lent the monks "a striking cheerfulness, so that one of them was asked, 'How it is that you are never downcast?' to which he replied, 'Because every day I hope to die.' Another said, 'The person who keeps death before his eyes at all times, easily overcomes dejection and crampedness of soul" (Ranke-Heinemann, 30). Thus the practice of daily keeping death before one's eyes expresses the longing "to be with our Lord in Paradise" (ibid., 41).

With the monks the yearning for death is also linked to a strong expectation of the parousia. The primitive church's belief that the end was near flared up again. Rufinus writes, "that the monks awaited the arrival of Christ as children await their father or an army its king or a true servant his lord and liberator. And in another passage: 'They take no more care for clothing and food, but only singing hymns they turn their hopes toward the Parousia of Christ'" (ibid., 32). The lightness and ease that we notice in many of the monastic fathers is surely connected with this expectation of the Second Coming. Hence Evagrius calls the monk a "high-flying eagle." Because the monks are waiting for the Lord, they become free of earthly cares, free of judgment and the expectations of others. Cheerful serenity, freedom, trust, and openness to each moment mark the monks who are longing for the Lord.

Many sayings of the fathers start out from the assumption that we must first die to the world in order to be up to the tasks that the world sets us: "A brother asked Father Moses, 'I see a task before me and I cannot fulfill it.' The old man said to him: 'If you do not become like a dead body, like those who are buried, you cannot master it.'"

If I completely identify with a job, if I make my sense of self-worth dependent on whether I can do it, then I will ultimately be unable to master it. The fixation on my task blocks me. I am not free to tackle it, because I absolutely have to get it right. Fear of failure prevents me from doing a good job. Dying means giving up identification with the task. Then I am free to do it well, because everything doesn't depend upon how I get it done. Dying to the world, or imagining that I am lying in my grave, expresses what transpersonal psychology nowadays calls disidentification: I look at my thoughts and feelings, but I don't identify with them. I see the tasks that I have to carry out, but I don't identify with them. I have a job, but I am not this job. I feel anger, but I am not my anger.

Psychosynthesis, developed by Roberto Assagioli, has worked out the method of disidentification. I look at my thoughts and feelings, for example, my fear. I sense this fear, but then I go back behind the fear to the un-moved witness, the untouched self. This inner core, the spiritual self, as Assagioli calls it, is untouched by fear and by the feelings that mark me in my emotional domain. Disidentification liberates me from the compulsion to have to carry out the task perfectly. For transpersonal psychology disidentification is true therapy. So long as we identify with a problem, it becomes permanent. We won't get really free from the problem until we stop identifying with it. "Disidentification from the ego, by which we recognize our true essence, is in transpersonal psychotherapy the most important prerequisite for our liberation" (Walsh, 187).

The method of disidentification is evident in yet another saying of the fathers: "A brother came to Father Makarios, the Egyptian, and said to him: 'Father, tell me something. How can I obtain salvation?' The old man taught him: 'Take a look at the tombstones and pour scorn on the dead.' So the brother went, jeered and threw stones at the graves. Then he came back and reported to the elder, who asked him: 'Didn't they say anything to you?' He answered: 'No.' Then the old man told him: 'Go there again tomorrow and praise them.' And he came to the old man and reported: 'I praised them.' And he asked: 'Didn't they answer?' The brother replied: 'No!' Then the elder taught him: 'You know how badly you abused them, and they didn't answer — and how much you praised them, and they said nothing to you. That is how you must be if you wish to find salvation. Be a corpse, heed neither the injustice of men nor their praise — like the dead, and you will be redeemed.'"

At first glance this method seems to be somewhat macabre, as if we were supposed to be as insensitive as the dead. But in truth the point is to transcend the level of identifying with praise and blame, to practice disidentification. According to this saying, our life succeeds only when we stop making ourselves totally dependent on praise and blame. For then we are never on our own. Another interesting point here is that the feelings of praise and blame are first acted out excessively before transcending the level of the feelings, before the young brother realizes that on that level he'll never find the way to success in life.

Becoming like the dead doesn't mean becoming insensible, but what happens in baptism: dying to the world, that is, human beings with their expectations and demands, their standards and judgments, have no more influence on us. We no longer identify with the world. We live beyond the threshold. We live in a spiritual reality, over which the world has no power. That makes us free. When we are constantly aiming to be praised, we will always remain discontented, because we are insatiable in our addiction to praise.

Makarios doesn't advise us to give up our need for praise completely. We can't do that. But we shouldn't identify ourselves with the praise or blame of others. We should sense that there is another reality in us, that we have a divine dignity, which is there whether people praise us or blame us. Only the experience of this divine dignity makes us free vis-à-vis praise and blame. So this is no renunciation we force upon ourselves, but the expression of our inner experience.

We are to be dead above all to those closest to us. "Father Poimen told this story: A brother asked Father Moses how a person could deaden himself toward his neighbor. The old man replied: 'Unless a person in his heart makes himself into someone who has been lying in the grave for three days, he will never acquire a spiritual attitude.' "

And from Father Moses we have the saying: "A person must be dead to his companion, so that he doesn't judge him on any matter." Therefore to be dead to those who are closest to us means above all to renounce judging them. I have no right to pass judgment on others. But being dead to our neighbor can also mean being independent of the problems of others, not identifying with their difficulties. Of course, this mustn't become inhuman, as if we had no interest in others. From the many sayings of the fathers where an elder becomes involved heart and soul with the questioner, comforts him, and straightens him out, we can see that the monks weren't aiming at harshness and insensibility, but at inner distance. So we read in one of the sayings: "Paesios, the brother of Father Poimen, once had a disagreement with someone outside his *kellion*. Father Poimen thought this wasn't right, so he arose and fled to Father Ammonas. He told him: 'Paesios, my brother, had enmity with someone, and it leaves me no peace.' Father Ammonas answered him: 'Poimen, are you still alive? Get up, sit yourself down in your *kellion*, and tell your heart: You have already been in the grave for a year.'"

Poimen identifies himself so closely with his brother that the latter's animosity toward another robs him of his peace. There are enough sayings by the fathers in which an elder mediates disputes. But here it's his own brother who is involved, and Poimen can't be unbiased. Hence Father Ammonas advises him to imagine that he has already been lying in the grave for a year. This thought gives him distance he needs from his brother. His brother is responsible for himself. Poimen should not make his brother's problems his own.

For every therapist distance from the problems of the patient is the prerequisite for being able to really help the other person. So Poimen first has to get some distance from his brother. Then he can freely decide whether he wants to help and intervene in the quarrel, or if he will release him and trust him to resolve the conflict responsibly on his own.

Being dead vis-à-vis the other is even viewed by Poimen as an indispensable condition for getting along well with the other brothers. In another saying it is reported that "Poimen became a monk along with six of his blood brothers. After the seven brothers had to flee from the Maziks, who killed many monks, they settled down in Tenenutis. Anub, one of the brothers, threw stones every morning at a stone idol in the pagan temple. In the evening he would beg the idol for forgiveness. When Poimen took him to task for this, Anub answered him: "I did it for your sake. You saw that I pelted the face of the image with stones. Did it speak or get angry?" When Poimen answered that of course it didn't answer, Anub explained his behavior: "We are seven brothers. If you want us to stay together, then let us become like this image. Whether it is reviled or revered, it doesn't move. But if you don't want to be that way, look, there are four gates in the temple; each one can go out whichever way he wishes."

All seven brothers stayed together and took Anub's advice; and so they lived the whole time in peace and quiet. The distance from their own needs and emotions created an atmosphere in which the brothers could live together. This wasn't an unfeeling atmosphere; this attitude helped to build a space for love and security, for mutual understanding and freedom, where each one could go his own way without the others constantly trying to lecture him.

For us such advice at first sounds rather strange. But in the final analysis it is the fulfillment of Jesus' words: "Unless a grain of wheat falls into the earth and dies, it remains alone; but if it dies, it bears much fruit. He who loves his life loses it, and he who hates his life in this world will keep it for eternal life" (John 12:24–25). We have to let go of ourselves and our ideas; then a space for new possibilities will open up for us. We have to let go of our neighbor; then real relationships will become possible. When one person in a partnership clings to the other, the relationship becomes in the long run impossible. A partnership can last only if each one frees and releases the other. Letting go, psychology tells us, is the prerequisite for a fulfilled life.

Contemplation as a Path of Healing

A person can't be healed within simply through discipline. Dealing with thoughts, along with concrete exercises, helps to calm the passions and make the soul healthy. But it takes contemplation to actually achieve that health. That was the monks' experience, and that is how Evagrius Ponticus described it.

Contemplation is pure prayer, prayer without respite, praying beyond thoughts and feelings, praying as oneness with God. Evagrius never tires of calling prayer the most beautiful present God has given humans. The dignity of human beings consists in the fact that we can become one with God in prayer.

"Is there anything better than passionate communion with God, and anything higher than living completely in God's presence? A prayer that is no longer deflected by anything is the highest thing that human beings can accomplish." "Prayer is the ascent of the mind to God."

In prayer one must first be free from one's passions, above all from anger and care. But then too one must leave behind pious thoughts. We are not supposed to be

reflecting on God, but to become one with God. Evagrius never tires of writing about this: "If someone has
become free from disrupting passions, that does not yet
mean that he can really pray. Perhaps he is only familiar
with the purest thoughts, but lets himself be seduced into
pondering them; then he is far from God."

"The Holy Spirit has compassion on our weakness and
often comes to us, although we are not worthy of him.
If he visits us, while we are praying to him out of love
for the truth, he fills us and helps us to let go of all the
thoughts and reflections that hold us captive, and so he
leads us on to spiritual prayer."

"Be watchful that during prayer you do not cling to
any ideas, but remain in deep silence. Only in this way
will he who takes pity on the ignorant visit such an
insignificant person as you and present you with the
greatest of all gifts, prayer."

"If you are really praying, there will arise in you a
deep feeling of trust. Angels will accompany you and
reveal to you the meaning of the whole of creation."

"Prayer is an activity that corresponds to the dignity
of the spirit; or, better yet, it corresponds to its nobler
and actual effect."

In contemplation, according to Evagrius, we reach a
state of deepest silence. We discover in ourselves a space
of pure silence. Evagrius calls this "God's place" or "the
vision of peace." In a letter to a friend he writes: "If the
intellect now by God's grace flees away from these things
[passions], and casts off the old man, then his own condition at the time of prayer appears to him like a sapphire,
of the color of heaven, which Scripture calls the place

of God, whom the elders of Israel saw on Mount Sinai (Exod. 24:10). It also calls this place the vision of peace; here one sees in himself the peace that is more exalted than all our understanding and that watches over our hearts. For in a pure heart another heaven is stamped, whose vision is light and whose place is ghostly, where — how wonderfully! — we contemplate the insights of the things in existence. And even the holy angels gather with those who are worthy."

In prayer we look upon our own light; indeed we become aware of our own nature, which is all light, participating in the light of God. In this place of God, in the place of peace in the interior of the soul, only God dwells. And there everything is whole. There, in the love of God, all the wounds that life has inflicted on us close up. There all thoughts about people who have hurt us fade away. There our passions are not allowed in, there people with their expectations, their opinions, and their judgments cannot reach us. There we become one with God. There we plunge into God's light, into God's peace, into God's love. That is the goal of the spiritual path.

The spiritual path of the early monks is, then, not a moral way, but a mystical, a mystagogical way, that leads us into God. That is why the writings of Evagrius breathe, not some sort of dour severity, but love, attentiveness, and joy over our calling, to be allowed to be one with God in prayer. One senses in his words the longing for God. To be able to pray undisturbed, without distraction, is the highest thing a human being can do; that is what the monks yearned for with all their hearts.

"Real prayer makes the monks like angels, for they urgently long to see their Father, who is in heaven." "Blessed is that mind that, praying without distraction, feels an ever deeper yearning for God."

"Do you really want to pray? Then stay far away from the things of this world. Let heaven be your homeland. There you should live not with words alone, but through angelic deeds and ever deeper knowledge of God."

For the monks the goal of the spiritual path is becoming one with the triune God. Evagrius calls that the contemplation of God. The way to this contemplation passes through the exodus from Egypt — from the dependence on sin — across the sojourn in the wilderness, where the monks struggle with the passions, into the Promised Land. There the monks experience contemplation of things, that is, they see their foundation, they recognize God in all things. Then they head up to Jerusalem, which for Evagrius is a symbol for the contemplation of bodiless, spiritual essences. And the goal of the spiritual way is Zion, an image of the contemplation of the Trinity. In the triune God humans come to themselves; they recognize their true nature.

If we translate Evagrius's teaching into our language, this means that the true therapy for our problems and wounds is prayer. In prayer, in contemplation we abolish the identification with our thoughts and feelings. Transpersonal psychology, as mentioned, sees in this disidentification true therapy. As long as we are tied down to our feelings, as long as we make ourselves totally dependent on our well-being, as long as we identify with our fear, with our jealousy, with our anger, with our depression, they will become a chronic problem that we can never get rid of.

Not until we sense that the actual reality lies deeper, that God is the profoundest reality, will we be free from our imprisonment in our problems. What transpersonal psychology has discovered as a way of relativizing our problems and liberating us from their power is formulated by Evagrius as a counsel for prayer:

"If you wish to pray in a perfect fashion, drop what has to do with the flesh, so that your glance may not be clouded over while you pray," and: "If you devote yourself to prayer, you must leave behind everything else that gives you joy. Only then will you come to pure prayer."

For transpersonal psychology the mystical path is also the path into which all therapy must flow. It's not enough just to handle our problems better. We aren't really healed until we have acknowledged our true nature, until we have learned with our hearts that we are not determined by our relationships, our problems, or our fears, that we are in contact with our spiritual selves and with the untouched image that God has of us. And relationships, feelings, and passions have no power over this spiritual self.

In prayer we are allowed to dive into the place of silence, where everything is already whole and complete, where we can sense a deep peace amid all insults and injuries.

Eleven

Gentleness as a Sign of the Spiritual Person

The goal of the spiritual path is not the great ascetic, not the indefatigable faster, not the consistent person, but the meek and gentle one. Evagrius continually mentions gentleness as a sign of spirituality. He challenges us to be like Moses, of whom Scripture says: "Now the man Moses was very meek, more than all the men that were on the face of the earth" (Num. 12:3).

"Let no one put trust in continence alone, I beg you! For it is not possible to build a house with a single stone, nor to complete a building with a single brick. An angry ascetic is a piece of dry wood, without fruit in the autumn, twice dead and uprooted. An irascible person will not see the morning star rise but instead will go to a place of no return, a dark and gloomy land, where no light shines and no human life is to be seen. Continence merely suppresses the body, but gentleness makes the intellect see!"

Evagrius keeps stressing that asceticism is not enough by itself for the spiritual path. Gentleness is crucial. It alone transforms a person's heart and opens it to God.

"Continence all by itself is like that foolish virgin, who was barred from the nuptial chamber because her oil had run out and her lamp was extinguished." And he makes another comparison: "Those who abstain from food and drink, but whose heart is stirring with unjustified anger, are like a ship on the high seas piloted by the demon of anger."

Evagrius also sees in David and in Jesus the realization of the sort of meekness we should imitate: "Tell me, why did Scripture, when it wished to praise Moses, set aside all the miraculous signs, and mention only meekness? ...David too, when he mentioned the virtue of meekness, begged to be found worthy of just this, when he said: 'Remember, Lord, David and all his meekness.' He doesn't mention that his knees were weak from fasting and his flesh (from a lack of oil) was dwindling away, and that he awoke and was like a sparrow that flies around the roofs, when he said: 'Remember, O Lord, David, and all his meekness.' Let us also learn to acquire the gentleness of him who said: 'I am gentle and lowly in heart' (Matt. 11:29) so that he may teach us his ways and bring us to life in the Kingdom of Heaven."

Gentleness is for Evagrius the source of knowledge of Christ. Without gentleness, we can read the Bible as much as we like and engage in the harshest ascetical practices, but we will never understand the mystery of Christ. Thus he writes to a disciple: "But above all don't forget gentleness and calm, which purify the soul and bring us close to the knowledge of Christ."

The knowledge of Christ is another expression for contemplation. Without gentleness there is no true contemplation. To Rufinus Evagrius writes: "For I am convinced that your gentleness has become a cause of great knowledge. No single virtue produces wisdom as gentleness does, for whose sake even Moses was praised as gentler than all other men. And I too beg to become and be called a disciple of the Gentle one."

Thus gentleness is a sign that we have understood Christ and followed him.

Here we catch sight of a kind of spirituality different from the one we met in the moral theology textbooks of the 1950s. The spirituality of the early monks is distinguished not by strictness, not by moralizing, nor by fear tactics, but by the encouragement of gentleness. Gentle persons are attractive to many people. They don't have to convince persons of different faiths of their orthodoxy; they have no need of proselytizing. Their gentleness is sufficient testimony for Christ. Anyone who encounters that gentleness meets Christ and will recognize him in it.

Gentleness and compassion are the criteria of genuine spirituality. If we view and judge contemporary forms of piety with these criteria, we will quickly realize which kinds derive from fear of the repressed shadow and which come from the spirit of Christ. Only when men and women have become gentle and merciful and deal compassionately with their fellow human beings do they bear witness to a spirituality that is in keeping with Christ. All other kinds may behave ever so piously, but they still derive from the spirit of fear and repressed passion. To that extent we can learn from the early monks to develop a spirituality that matches the spirit of Christ.

Conclusion

To many people today the sayings of the fathers and the writings of the early monks may look like a strange and distant world. It is not always simple to feel our way into this language, so different from ours. But once we have discovered the wisdom that inhabits the words of the monastic fathers, we will not easily let them go. They are a treasure trove not just for the spiritual life, but also for psychology, which finds here the expression in a different vocabulary of what it has laboriously worked out only in this century. The difference between monastic and modern psychology is that the monks have tested what they say through their experience; they aren't developing theoretical models, but "merely" reflecting on their own experience.

A friend of mine, who as a psychologist takes continuing education courses, in which he studies fascinating new models of the mind, once told me: "We're constantly finding out about new psychological methods and explanatory models, but nobody thinks of really living them. There's no time for it. That's why your life interests me. What happens when one lives for decades according to this sort of model?"

The monks wished to introduce readers to a path that

was to be followed concretely and consistently. They always give a rather chilly reception when people come to them wanting to be edified by their wisdom, but unwilling to live it too. Thus Father Theodoros refused to say a word to a brother who had come to him. When a disciple reproached him for this, he replied: "Really, I didn't want to talk to him. He's a pompous individual who likes to boast with strange words."

Words are useless if they aren't lived. That's what Father Jacob says in yet another passage: "One needs to do more than talk. For there is a great deal of talking among people these days. What's needed is action. That is what one looks for, not speeches that bear no fruit."

What we can learn from the monks is the *longing for God,* the longing that goads us to go off into the wilderness, to struggle consistently with our passions, to faithfully persevere with our ascetical practice. The monks yearn to experience God, to become one with God. For the sake of God they leave the world; for the sake of God they take the struggle upon themselves. They have obviously tasted God, and so they don't slacken until they have found God. One elder compares the monk to a dog that has the taste of the hare in his mouth and won't give up until he has caught it: "A monk should observe the dogs on the hunt for hares. Only the one that has seen the hare chases it, while the others that have seen that dog run after him, but only so long as they don't get tired, and then suddenly they turn back. And only the first one, who actually saw the hare, continues the chase until he has caught it and will not be held back in his chase (while the others have abandoned theirs), neither by chasms, forests, nor thickets, neither by scratching thorns or wounds. He will not give up until he seizes the hare. And so the monk who seeks Christ the Lord should unceasingly look upon the cross and ignore all the troubles that come his way until he has reached the Crucified."

The goal of the struggle, the hunt, the way, is God. The monks do not give up until they have found God, until they can pray without distraction, until with all their thoughts and emotions they are directed to God and find in God the fulfillment of all their longing. If we, like the dog hunting the hare, have the taste of God in our mouth, then we won't let ourselves be discouraged on our spiritual path, neither by the continual conflicts within the church, nor by the widespread depressiveness that marks our society, nor by the secularization of our time, in which there are often so few traces of God. It is not the achiever's mentality that spurs us on the way to God, but God himself, whom we have once tasted and whose taste won't leave us until we have found him.

Nowadays the monastic fathers could show us a way out of the superficial debates about the structure of the church or the exhaustion of spirituality. They invite us onto the path of longing. The longing for God sends us off through all obstacles on the chase for the hare, for oneness with God, for the coming of Jesus Christ, "who will change our lowly body to be like his glorious body" (Phil. 3:21).

The striving of the monks ultimately aims at fulfilling the biblical command to "pray without ceasing" (1 Thess. 5:17). The great question of the monks is how to do just this, how they can direct their whole effort toward God. With all their words, with the experiences that they have had, with the struggles they have endured, they wish to invite us to set off on the path to God until we can pray without ceasing and in prayer experience our true dignity.

It is the voice of the early church that calls out to us in the monks: "Pray all the time, because only prayer makes you a complete person, and only through prayer do you discover your full dignity. But most especially prayer will deepen your love for God. It will become stronger and stronger until the day when you will see what you have longed for in prayer."

But the path to God passes through our own reality, through observation of our thoughts, through proper dealing with the passions, and through an ascetical practice that will train us for openness to God. It is a *spirituality from below* that the monks teach us, a spirituality that has the courage to look upon everything that is in us and offer it to God. They invite us to take the path of humility, on which we ascend to God by climbing down into our own reality. The model is Jesus himself, who came down from heaven to carry us up to God as his brothers and sisters. For Paul too this is our way: only those who have first gone down can ascend to God (see Eph. 4:9–10).

We will come to God only on a path that goes through sincere self-encounter, through listening to our thoughts and feelings, to our dreams, to our body, our concrete lives, and our relationships with other people. And God will transform everything that we hold out to him, until the image of Jesus Christ shines out in us too, the image that God has pictured to himself of every single one of us and that can irradiate the world only in and through us. All the pains that the monks have taken in their asceticism have no other aim but to make this unique image of God appear in this world without distortion.

The monks wish to pass on to us today their optimism, their confidence that we can work on ourselves, that we are not incurably abandoned to our predispositions or our education or the current social situation, but that it's worthwhile to form ourselves through asceticism until the image of God shines out undimmed from us, and until the unique word that God speaks through every one of us rings out clearly in our world.

The dignity of every individual who was formed by God in a unique way and in each of whom God speaks a different word, peculiar to you and me, is the reason why the monks invite us to the ascetical life. We should and can work on ourselves. We can find our true self — and we will find God, who in prayer and contemplation heals our deepest wounds and silences the longing of our hearts.

Bibliography

Athanasius. *Leben des heiligen Antonius.* Trans. H. Mertel. Kempten and Munich, 1917.

Ausgewählte Schriften der syrischen Kirchenväter. Trans. Gustav Bickell. Kempten, 1874.

Des hl. Abtes Dorotheus Geistliche Gespräche. Trans. B. Hermann. Kevlaer, 1928.

Evagrius Ponticus. *Antirrheticus magnus: Die große Widerrede.* Trans. Leo Trunk. Manuscript. Münsterschwarzach, 1992.

———. *Briefe aus der Wüste.* Trans. and intro. Gabriel Bunge. Würzburg, 1992.

———. *Praktikos: Über das Gebet.* Trans. and intro. J. E. Bamberger. Münsterschwarzach, 1986.

Gruen, Anselm. *Einreden: Der Umgang mit den Gedanken.* Münsterschwarzach, 1982.

———. *Bilder von Verwandlung.* Münsterschwarzach, 1986.

———. *Geistliche Begleitung bei den Wüstenvätern.* Münsterschwarzach, 1991.

———. *Der Umgang mit dem Bösen: Der Dämonenkampf im alten Mönchtum.* Münsterschwarzach, 1993.

Heussi, Karl. *Der Ursprung des Mönchtums.* Tübingen, 1926.

John Cassian. *Spannkraft der Seele.* Selected and trans. Gertrude and Thomas Sartory. Freiburg, 1982.

Kästner, Erhart. *Die Stundentrommel vom Heiligen Berg Athos.* Wiesbaden, 1956.

Lebenshilfe aus der Wüste: Die alten Mönchsväter als Therapeuten. Selected and trans. Gertrude and Thomas Sartory. Freiburg, 1980.

Les sentences des pères du désert. 3d collection. Ed. L. Regnault. Solesmes, 1976.

Les sentences des pères du désert. New collection. Ed. L. Regnault. Solesmes, 1977.

Ranke-Heinemann, Uta. *Das frühe Mönchtum: Seine Motive nach den Selbstzeugnissen.* Essen, 1964.

Smolitsch, Igor. *Leben und Lehre der Starzen.* Vienna, 1936.

Sprücher der Väter (Apophthegmata Patrum). Trans. P. Bonifatius. Graz, 1963.

Walsh, Roger N., and Frances Vaughn. *Psychologie in der Wende.* Munich, 1985.

Weisung der Väter. Trans. B. Miller. 3d ed. Trier, 1986.